God Beyond Existence

God Beyond Existence

A Comparative Exploration of Ultimate Reality

CONDE CAGALITAN

RESOURCE *Publications* • Eugene, Oregon

GOD BEYOND EXISTENCE
A Comparative Exploration of Ultimate Reality

Resource Publications
An Imprint of Wipf and Stock Publishers
199 W. 8th Ave., Suite 3
Eugene, OR 97401

www.wipfandstock.com

PAPERBACK ISBN: 979-8-3852-7982-1
HARDCOVER ISBN: 979-8-3852-7983-8
EBOOK ISBN: 979-8-3852-7984-5

VERSION NUMBER 06/18/26

Dedication

To the One beyond all names,
whose nearness is the beginning of all knowing,
whose presence precedes existence,
and whose quiet voice has followed me through every threshold of thought.
To the Designer who called the mind into being,
who waited patiently at the edge of my understanding,
and who revealed that truth is not discovered but received.
And to every soul who senses, even faintly,
that there is more than the world has taught them to expect—
may these pages guide you toward the Center that has always known your name.

Contents

Preface

THIS BOOK BEGAN AS a question that refused to leave me: What lies beyond existence itself? Not as an abstraction, nor as a theological slogan, but as a genuine inquiry into the ground from which all things arise. Every tradition I encountered—philosophical, religious, mystical, and scientific—seemed to gesture toward something deeper than the world of forms, yet none could fully name it without reducing it.

The chapters that follow are the result of tracing that question across the landscapes of metaphysics, consciousness, and comparative theology. They are not an attempt to harmonize traditions or to collapse differences, but to listen for the underlying structure that makes their insights possible. What emerged was not a system imposed from above, but a pattern revealed from within: the Real as the ground of all existence, the silent foundation that sustains God, self, and world.

This work does not argue for a doctrine, nor does it seek to persuade by authority. Its method is simple: to follow the logic of being to its limit, to examine the transparency of existence, and to allow the Real to disclose itself through the very conditions that make understanding possible. The comparative elements are offered not as proofs, but as mirrors—each tradition illuminating a different facet of the same depth.

Readers will notice that this book moves between philosophical clarity and contemplative stillness. That is intentional. The inquiry into ultimate reality is never merely intellectual; it is also experiential, existential, and transformative. To ask what lies beyond existence is to confront the ground of one's own being.

If these pages serve any purpose, let it be this: to help the reader recognize the quiet nearness of the Real—the One who precedes all names, sustains all knowing, and calls every soul toward the Center from which it came.

CONDE CAGALITAN
Sydney, 2026

Introduction

Every serious inquiry into ultimate reality begins with a simple intuition: that the world, as it appears, is not selfexplanatory. Beneath the movement of forms, beneath the shifting patterns of thought and experience, there is a depth that cannot be reduced to matter, language, or perception. Philosophers have named this depth in many ways—Being, the Absolute, Brahman, the Tao, the Ground—but each name gestures toward something that exceeds the limits of existence itself.

This book enters that ancient conversation with a single guiding conviction: that the Real, the ground of all that exists, is not a being among beings but the condition that makes being possible. To speak of God, self, or world without acknowledging this deeper foundation is to mistake the surface for the source. The task of metaphysics is not to construct a system but to uncover the structure that already holds everything together.

The chapters that follow explore this structure through a comparative lens. They draw from classical metaphysics, nondual traditions, philosophical theology, and contemporary reflections on consciousness—not to merge them into a single doctrine, but to reveal the shared intuition that runs through them. Each tradition offers a different angle of approach, a different vocabulary, a different way of naming the depth that precedes existence. When placed side by side, these perspectives illuminate one another, revealing a pattern that no single tradition can fully articulate on its own.

This exploration is not merely theoretical. To ask what lies beyond existence is to confront the ground of one's own being. It is to recognize that the self is not an isolated center of awareness but an expression of a deeper unity that sustains all things. The inquiry into ultimate reality is therefore also an inquiry into the nature of consciousness, identity, and the world we inhabit. It is a philosophical journey, but it is also an existential one.

Readers will find that this book moves between clarity and contemplation, between analysis and stillness. This is intentional. The Real cannot be captured by concepts alone, yet concepts can guide the mind toward the threshold where understanding becomes recognition. The aim is not to define the Real but to make its presence intelligible—to show how it grounds every moment of experience, every act of knowing, every form that appears.

If this book succeeds, it will not be because it offers new answers, but because it helps the reader see the ancient questions with fresh eyes. The Real has always been near. The task is simply to notice.

1

EXISTENCE

HUMAN BEINGS SPEAK OF existence as if it were the most obvious thing in the world. We say that mountains exist, that stars exist, that atoms exist, that thoughts exist, that people exist. We treat existence as a universal category, a container large enough to hold everything that is real. Yet the moment we turn this category toward God, something fractures. The word that seemed so stable suddenly collapses under its own weight.

Existence is not a neutral word. It is a human word, shaped by human experience, bound to the conditions of the world we inhabit. It is a word that belongs to time, to space, to matter, to change, to limitation. Everything we call "existing" is something that began, something that is sustained, something that depends on something else. Existence, as we know it, is always contingent.

This is the first threshold of the book: *to recognise that existence is not an absolute category*. It is a created category. It describes the condition of things that are not selfsustaining, not eternal, not infinite. Existence is the realm of the dependent.

And this raises the central question:

Can God be placed inside a category that belongs only to created things?

c relation to other things. A tree exists because it grows, takes up space, casts a shadow, and eventually dies. A star exists because it burns, emits light, and collapses. A thought exists because it arises in consciousness and then fades.

But none of these conditions can be applied to God without reducing God to a creature.

If God is the source of all things, then God cannot be one thing among others. If God is the ground of being, then God cannot be a being. If God is the cause of existence, then God cannot be placed inside the category of existence.

To say "God exists" is to use a word that is too small.

This is not a denial of God. It is a recognition that the human category of existence is inadequate for the One who gives existence to all things.

EXISTENCE AS A HUMAN LENS

Existence is not a property of God; it is a property of creation. It is the condition of everything that is not God. When we speak of existence, we are speaking from within the human experience of reality—an experience shaped by:

- birth and death
- change and decay
- time and sequence
- space and limitation
- cause and effect

These are the boundaries of the human world. They are the conditions under which we live, think, and speak. But they are not the conditions of God.

To speak of God as "existing" is to assume that God shares our conditions. It is to imagine God as a larger, more powerful version of ourselves—a being who lives inside the same framework we do, only higher up the chain.

This is the root of the problem.

We mistake the human lens for the universal lens.

THE CATEGORY ERROR

When we ask, "Does God exist?" we are already making a category error. We are treating God as if God were an object inside the universe, subject to the same rules as everything else. But God is not an object. God is not a thing. God is not a member of the set of existing entities.

God is the source of the set.

This is why the question "Does God exist?" is fundamentally flawed. It is like asking:

"What colour is the number seven?"

"How heavy is justice?"

"Where does the horizon live?"

The question fails because the categories do not match.

God is not something that exists.

God is the One through whom existence itself becomes possible.

THE HUMAN NEED FOR CATEGORIES

Human beings cannot think without categories. We divide reality into shapes, names, concepts, and definitions. We do this not because reality is divided, but because the mind cannot grasp the whole. Existence is one of these categories—a mental tool that helps us navigate the world.

But tools have limits.

A hammer is useful for nails, but not for water. A net is useful for fish, but not for wind. Existence is useful for describing created things, but not for describing the Creator.

The moment we apply the category of existence to God, we reduce God to something less than God. We shrink the Infinite into the finite. We compress the Eternal into the temporal. We force the Unbounded into the boundaries of human thought.

This is why the mystics of every tradition insist that God is beyond being, beyond existence, beyond all categories.

THE THRESHOLD OF UNKNOWING

To approach God, we must first recognise the limits of our own language. We must acknowledge that existence is a human word, not a divine one. We must let go of the assumption that our categories can contain the One who transcends them.

This is the threshold of unknowing—the point where human language reaches its limit and must fall silent. Not because God is absent, but because God is too present. Not because God is unknowable, but because God is known in a way that surpasses the mind.

Existence is the first veil.

To lift it is to begin the journey toward the Real.

SUMMARY OF THE CHAPTER

Existence is a human category, not a divine one.

Everything that exists is contingent, dependent, and limited.

God, as the source of all being, cannot be placed inside the category of existence.

The question "Does God exist?" is a category error.

Human language and categories cannot contain the Infinite.

To approach God, we must recognise the limits of existence as a concept.

This chapter establishes the foundation for everything that follows. Once existence is understood as a limited human category, the next question naturally arises:

If existence is inadequate, what about the other categories we use—time, space, language, and understanding?

2

TIME AND SPACE

HUMAN BEINGS LIVE INSIDE time and space so completely that we rarely question them. We wake, move, work, age, and sleep within a sequence of moments. We occupy bodies that take up space, move through space, and depend on space to exist. Time and space feel absolute because they define the boundaries of our experience. Yet these boundaries are not universal. They are not divine. They are not eternal. They are the conditions of creation, not the conditions of God.

To understand why God cannot be placed inside the category of existence, we must first understand the deeper truth: *God cannot be placed inside time or space either.* These two frameworks shape everything we know, but they do not shape the One who made them.

TIME AS A CREATED SEQUENCE

Time is not an independent reality. It is a sequence of moments that arise only within creation. Time is the measurement of change—the movement from one state to another, from potential to actual, from becoming to being. Everything that exists within the universe is subject to time because everything changes.

But God does not change.

If God changed, God would move from one state to another, which would imply imperfection. If God learned, God would have lacked knowledge. If God grew, God would have been incomplete. If God diminished, God would cease to be God.

Time is the measure of change.

God is changeless.

Therefore, God is not in time.

This is why the ancient traditions speak of God as eternal—not meaning "endless time," but *timelessness.* Eternity is not infinite duration; it is the absence of duration. It is the state in which all moments are present, not sequential.

To say "God exists in time" is to reduce God to a creature.

SPACE AS A CREATED DIMENSION

Space, like time, is a created framework. It is the dimension in which physical objects have shape, form, and location. Space allows things to be separate from one another. It allows distance, direction, and movement.

But God is not an object.

God does not occupy a location.

God is not "somewhere."

If God were located in space, God would be limited by space. God would be here and not there. God would be contained. God would be measurable. God would be finite.

But the Infinite cannot be contained.

This is why the mystics say that God is "everywhere and nowhere," not because God is spread out like a gas, but because God is not spatial at all. God is not extended. God is not located. God is not bound by dimension.

Space is the condition of bodies.

God is not a body.

Therefore, God is not in space.

THE HUMAN EXPERIENCE OF TIME AND SPACE

Human beings cannot imagine a reality without time or space because our minds are shaped by them. Every thought we have is sequential. Every perception we have is spatial. Even our language is structured by time and space:

- before and after
- here and there
- cause and effect
- near and far
- beginning and end

These are not universal categories. They are human categories. They describe the world we inhabit, not the One who created it.

This is why every attempt to imagine God "before creation" fails. The word "before" is a time-word. It assumes a sequence. But time itself begins with creation. There is no "before" creation, because "before" is a temporal concept.

Likewise, every attempt to imagine God "outside the universe" fails. The word "outside" is a space-word. It assumes location. But space itself begins with creation. There is no "outside" of space, because "outside" is a spatial concept.

We are trying to use tools that belong to creation to describe the Creator.

THE COLLAPSE OF HUMAN CATEGORIES

When we say "God is eternal," we imagine infinite time.

When we say "God is omnipresent," we imagine infinite space.

When we say "God is infinite," we imagine endless extension.

But these are human projections.

Eternity is not infinite time.

Omnipresence is not infinite space.

Infinity is not endless extension.

These are metaphors—attempts to stretch human categories beyond their limits. But even stretched, they remain human categories. They cannot contain the Infinite.

This is why the mystics insist that God is beyond time and beyond space. Not because God is distant, but because God is the source of both. Time and space are expressions of the divine, not boundaries around the divine.

THE ILLUSION OF DIVINE SEQUENCE

When people imagine God acting, they imagine sequence:

- God decides
- then God speaks
- then God creates
- then God responds
- then God judges

But this is human language describing divine action. It is not literal. God does not move from one moment to another. God does not wait. God does not anticipate. God does not react.

All divine action is eternal.

All divine knowledge is immediate.

All divine presence is simultaneous.

The sequence is in our perception, not in God.

THE THRESHOLD OF TRANSCENDENCE

To approach God, we must recognise that time and space are not universal realities. They are created frameworks that shape human experience but do not shape the Creator. God is not inside time or space. God is the One through whom time and space come into being.

This is the second veil.

To lift it is to see that God is not a being within the universe, but the ground of the universe itself.

SUMMARY OF THE CHAPTER

- Time and space are created frameworks, not divine attributes.
- God is not in time because God does not change.
- God is not in space because God is not a body.
- Human perception is shaped by time and space, but God is not.
- Divine action is eternal, not sequential.
- Time and space collapse as categories when applied to God.

3

ULTIMATE REALITY

Human beings have always sensed that beneath the shifting surface of the world lies something deeper, something stable, something unchanging. Every culture, every religion, every philosophical tradition has reached toward this intuition in its own way. The names differ, the metaphors differ, the languages differ, but the impulse is the same: to point toward the *Ultimate Reality* that grounds all things.

This chapter explores that Reality—not as a concept, not as a doctrine, but as the unconditioned foundation of everything that is. It is the Reality that cannot be divided, cannot be compared, cannot be placed alongside anything else. It is the Reality that precedes all categories, including existence, time, and space.

Ultimate Reality is not one being among many.

Ultimate Reality is the *source* of being itself.

THE HUMAN INTUITION OF THE REAL

Across history, humans have sensed that the world of appearances is not the whole story. The world changes, decays, and dissolves, yet something persists beneath the flux. This intuition appears everywhere:

- In the philosopher's search for the unchanging.
- In the mystic's longing for union.
- In the scientist's search for fundamental laws.
- In the poet's sense of the eternal.

This intuition is not an argument; it is an awareness. It is the quiet recognition that the world points beyond itself.

- The ancient Greeks called it *to on*—the Being behind beings.
- The Hindus called it *Brahman*—the Absolute.
- The Taoists called it *the Tao*—the Way that cannot be named.
- The Hebrews called it *Ehyeh Asher Ehyeh*—"I Am Who I Am."
- The mystics called it the Real, the One, the Infinite.

Different names, same intuition:
There is a Reality that is not conditioned by anything else.

THE REAL BEYOND CONCEPTS

Ultimate Reality cannot be captured by concepts because concepts divide. To define something is to place boundaries around it, to say what it is and what it is not. But the Real has no boundaries. It cannot be divided into parts. It cannot be compared to anything else. It cannot be placed in opposition to anything.

Concepts belong to the mind.

The Real is prior to the mind.

This is why the Upanishads say, "Neti, neti"—"Not this, not that."

This is why the Tao Te Ching begins, "The Tao that can be spoken is not the eternal Tao."

This is why the mystics speak of the "cloud of unknowing."

Ultimate Reality is not an object of thought.

It is the ground of thought.

THE UNITY BENEATH DIVERSITY

The world appears diverse—countless forms, countless beings, countless experiences. But diversity is the surface. Beneath it lies unity. Every tradition has expressed this in its own way:

- The ocean and its waves.
- The sun and its rays.
- The tree and its branches.
- The fire and its sparks.

The metaphors differ, but the truth is the same:
Multiplicity emerges from unity.
The Real is not one thing among many.
The Real is the One from which the many arise.

This unity is not numerical. It is not the "first" in a sequence. It is not a member of a set. It is the condition for all sets, all sequences, all numbers.

Unity is not a quantity.
Unity is the nature of the Real.

THE REAL AS UNCONDITIONED

Everything in the universe is conditioned:

- by time
- by space
- by cause
- by relation
- by form
- by limitation

But the Real is unconditioned.

It depends on nothing.
It is caused by nothing.
It is limited by nothing.
This is why the Real cannot be described.
To describe something is to condition it.
To condition something is to limit it.
To limit something is to make it finite.
The Real is infinite not because it is large, but because it is unbounded.

THE COLLAPSE OF DUALITY

Human thought is dualistic. We think in opposites:

- light and dark
- good and evil
- being and non-being
- self and other
- sacred and profane

But these dualities belong to the human mind, not to the Real.
The Real is not divided.
The Real is not two.
The Real is not even "one" in the numerical sense.
The Real is beyond duality.
Beyond opposition.
Beyond comparison.
This is why the mystics speak of non-duality—not as a doctrine, but as a recognition that the Real cannot be split.

THE REAL AS THE GROUND OF ALL THINGS

Ultimate Reality is not something separate from the world. It is the ground of the world. It is the foundation upon which all things stand. It is the source from which all things arise. It is the presence that sustains all things.

The Real is not "out there."

The Real is the condition for "here" and "there."

The Real is not "before creation."

The Real is the condition for "before" and "after."

The Real is not "beyond the universe."

The Real is the condition for "beyond" and "within."

The Real is not a being.

The Real is Being-itself.

THE THRESHOLD OF ULTIMATE REALITY

To approach Ultimate Reality, we must let go of the assumption that the world of appearances is the whole story. We must recognise that the categories we use—existence, time, space, form, concept—are not universal. They are human. They describe the world we inhabit, not the Reality that grounds it.

Ultimate Reality is not hidden.

It is not distant.

It is not absent.

It is the most intimate presence, the foundation of every moment, the ground of every breath, the source of every thought.

The Real is not something we find.

It is something we awaken to.

SUMMARY OF THE CHAPTER

- Ultimate Reality is the unconditioned ground of all things.
- Every tradition points toward this Reality in its own way.
- Concepts cannot contain the Real.
- Unity lies beneath all diversity.
- The Real is beyond duality and beyond comparison.

- The Real is not a being but the source of being.
- To approach the Real is to awaken to what has always been present.

4

THE UNIFIED SOURCE OF REALITY

Human beings perceive the world as a collection of separate things. We see mountains and oceans, stars and atoms, animals and people, thoughts and emotions. Everything appears divided, distinct, and independent. Yet beneath this surface of multiplicity lies a deeper truth: *all things emerge from a single Source*. This Source is not one being among many. It is not a part of the universe. It is not a force within nature. It is the ground from which nature itself arises.

To speak of a unified Source is not to introduce another object into the universe. It is to recognise that the universe itself is grounded in something prior to it—something unconditioned, indivisible, and absolute. This chapter explores that Source, not as a theological claim, but as a metaphysical necessity.

THE ILLUSION OF SEPARATION

The human mind divides reality into parts because it must. Perception works by contrast. Thought works by distinction. Language works by separation. We cannot think without dividing. We cannot speak without naming. We cannot perceive without boundaries.

But these boundaries are not ultimate. They are functional. They help us navigate the world, but they do not describe the world as it truly is.

The ocean appears as countless waves, yet the waves are not separate from the ocean. The branches of a tree appear distinct, yet they arise from the same trunk. Light appears as many colours, yet all colours emerge from a single source.

Multiplicity is the appearance.

Unity is the reality.

THE SOURCE AS THE GROUND OF ALL THINGS

Every effect has a cause. Every form has an origin. Every contingent thing depends on something else. This chain of dependence cannot extend infinitely in the realm of conditioned things. There must be a foundation—a ground that does not depend on anything else.

This ground is the unified Source.

It is not a first cause in a temporal sequence.

It is not "before" creation.

It is not "outside" the universe.

It is the *condition* for all causes, all sequences, all locations.

The Source is not something that exists.

The Source is that through which existence becomes possible.

THE ONE BEYOND THE MANY

Across cultures, the intuition of a unified Source appears again and again:

- In Neoplatonism, it is *The One*—beyond being, beyond thought.
- In Hindu philosophy, it is *Brahman*—the Absolute, the unconditioned Real.
- In Islamic theology, it is *tawhid*—the radical unity of God.
- In Christian mysticism, it is the *Ground of Being*.
- In Taoism, it is the *Tao*—the nameless origin of heaven and earth.

These traditions differ in language, but converge in insight: *the many arise from the One.*
The One is not numerical.
It is not the first in a series.
It is the indivisible foundation of all series.

THE SOURCE AS NON-BEING AND BEYOND-BEING

To call the Source "being" is to limit it.
To call it "non-being" is also to limit it.
The Source is beyond both.
Being belongs to things that exist.
Non-being belongs to things that do not exist.
The Source is prior to both categories.
This is why the mystics speak in paradox:

- "God is nothing—not because God does not exist, but because God is no thing."
- "The One is beyond being."
- "The Real is neither being nor non-being."

These statements are not contradictions. They are attempts to point beyond the limits of language.

THE SOURCE AS THE ORIGIN OF FORM AND MEANING

Everything that exists has form—shape, structure, identity. But form is not self-generated. It arises from a deeper order. The Source is not a form, but the origin of all forms. It is not a meaning, but the origin of all meaning.

This is why the ancient traditions speak of the Source as:

- light
- life
- truth
- wisdom
- order
- harmony

These are metaphors, not descriptions. They point to the fact that the Source is the ground of intelligibility. Without the Source, nothing could be known, named, or understood.

The Source is not an object of knowledge.

It is the condition for knowledge.

THE SOURCE AS THE SILENT CENTER

The closer one approaches the Source, the more language fails. Concepts dissolve. Distinctions collapse. The mind reaches its limit. What remains is a silent awareness—a recognition that the Source is not something to be grasped, but something to be realised.

This is why the mystics speak of:

- stillness
- silence
- emptiness
- fullness
- union
- presence

These are not states of mind. They are glimpses of the Real.

The Source is not distant.

It is the silent center of all things.

THE THRESHOLD OF THE UNIFIED SOURCE

To recognise the unified Source is to see that the world is not a collection of separate things, but a single reality expressing itself in countless forms. It is to see that the boundaries we perceive are functional, not ultimate. It is to see that the Source is not an object within the universe, but the ground of the universe itself.

This recognition prepares the reader for the next movement of the book:

If the Source is unified and unconditioned, then *how did human beings come to speak about it?*

Where did language come from?

How did we begin naming the Real?

This leads naturally into the next chapter:

The Origin of Language: Scriptural Revelation.

SUMMARY OF THE CHAPTER

- The world appears divided, but arises from a single Source.
- The Source is not a being, but the ground of being.
- The Source is unconditioned, indivisible, and beyond all categories.
- Multiplicity is the appearance; unity is the reality.
- The Source is the origin of all form, meaning, and intelligibility.
- Language collapses at the threshold of the Source.
- Recognising the Source prepares us to explore the origins of language.

5

THE ORIGIN OF LANGUAGE

Scriptural Revelation

HUMAN LANGUAGE DID NOT begin as a human invention. Long before people shaped words with their tongues, long before tribes formed grammar, long before cultures carved symbols into clay or inked them onto scrolls, language appears in the oldest stories of humanity as something *given*, not created. In the scriptural imagination of the ancient world, language is not a tool humans discovered—it is a gift humans received.

This chapter explores the scriptural claim that language originates in the divine. It is not merely a means of communication but a medium of creation, revelation, and relationship. In the scriptural worldview, language is not human speech about God; it is God's speech to humanity.

THE FIRST VOICE IN SCRIPTURE IS NOT HUMAN

The opening line of Genesis is not a human voice. It is not a human thought. It is not a human word. The first voice in the biblical story is divine:

"And God said. . ."

Creation begins with speech.

Light appears because God speaks.

Order emerges because God speaks.

Life unfolds because God speaks.

In this worldview, language is not a human achievement. It is the *instrument of creation*. The universe is not built with hands; it is spoken into being. Reality itself is articulated.

This is the first scriptural claim about language:

Language is older than humanity.

DIVINE SPEECH AS CREATIVE POWER

In the scriptural imagination, speech is not descriptive—it is generative. God does not describe the world; God calls it forth. The divine word is not commentary; it is causation.

This is why the Hebrew word *dabar* means both "word" and "action."

A divine word is not a sound; it is an event.

- When God speaks, something happens.
- When God names, something becomes.
- When God commands, something emerges.

Language, in this view, is not a symbol pointing to reality.

Language is the force that *brings reality into being.*

THE LOGOS: LANGUAGE AS DIVINE REASON

In the Christian tradition, the Gospel of John deepens this idea:

"In the beginning was the Word (Logos)...

and the Word was God."

Here, the "Word" is not a sound but the divine logic, the ordering principle of reality, the rational structure through which all things come into being. The Logos is the bridge between the unconditioned Source and the conditioned world.

This is not metaphor.

It is metaphysics.
The universe is intelligible because it is spoken.
Reality is coherent because it is articulated.
Meaning exists because the Source is not silent.

REVELATION AS RECEIVED LANGUAGE

Scripture consistently portrays language as something *received*, not invented. Prophets do not create their messages; they hear them. They do not craft divine speech; they transmit it.

- "The word of the Lord came to. . ."
- "Thus says the Lord. . ."
- "Hear, O Israel. . ."
- "The Spirit spoke. . ."

In these traditions, revelation is not a human attempt to reach God.
Revelation is God's attempt to reach humanity.

LANGUAGE FLOWS DOWNWARD, NOT UPWARD.

This is why sacred texts are treated not as human reflections on the divine but as divine communication to the human. The words are not merely inspired; they are given.

THE SACREDNESS OF THE SPOKEN WORD

In ancient cultures, the spoken word carried a weight modern people often forget. Words were not casual. Words were not disposable. Words were believed to shape reality, bind agreements, bless, curse, heal, or destroy.

To speak was to act.
To name was to define.
To declare was to establish.
This is why divine speech is central to scripture.

It is not symbolic.
It is not poetic.
It is ontological.
Language is the bridge between the Infinite and the finite.

THE HUMAN RECEPTION OF DIVINE LANGUAGE

If language originates in God, then human language is a *derivative*—a reflection, an echo, a participation in the divine speech. Humans speak because they are spoken to. Humans name because they are named. Humans communicate because they are addressed.

This is why the first human words in Genesis are responses, not initiations.

Human speech begins as *answering.*
Human language is dialogical.
It begins in relationship.
It begins in being called.
This is the scriptural anthropology of language:
To be human is to be addressed.

THE COLLAPSE OF DIVINE LANGUAGE INTO HUMAN LANGUAGE

Over time, divine language becomes human language. The sacred becomes ordinary. The revelatory becomes functional. Words that once carried cosmic weight become tools for survival, trade, politics, and daily life.

But the scriptural memory remains:
Language is not merely human.
It is rooted in the divine.

This memory becomes crucial for the later chapters of the book, because it reveals a tension:

- God's speech is perfect.
- Human speech is limited.
- God's word creates.
- Human words distort.

This tension becomes the foundation for the later question: *How can human language ever speak truthfully about God?*

THE THRESHOLD OF SCRIPTURAL LANGUAGE

To understand God, we must understand language.

To understand language, we must understand its origin.

And in the scriptural worldview, the origin of language is not human ingenuity but divine generosity.

Language is revelation.

Language is creation.

Language is relationship.

This chapter prepares the reader for the next step:

If language begins in God, how did it evolve in human history?

How did humans develop the capacity to speak, name, and conceptualize?

This leads naturally into the next chapter:

The Origin of Language—Human Development and History.

Summary of the Chapter

- Scripture presents language as divine in origin.
- God speaks creation into being.
- The Logos is the rational structure of reality.
- Revelation is received, not invented.
- Human language is a derivative of divine speech.
- Language begins in relationship—humans are addressed before they speak.
- The sacred origin of language sets the stage for understanding its limitations.

6

THE ORIGIN OF LANGUAGE

Human Development and History

IF CHAPTER 5 REVEALED language as a divine gift in the scriptural imagination, Chapter 6 turns to the human story—the long, slow evolution of symbols, sounds, and meaning. Human language did not appear suddenly. It emerged through millennia of cognitive development, social cooperation, and the growing complexity of human life. This chapter explores that evolution, not to contradict the scriptural view, but to complement it. The divine and the human are not competing explanations; they are two perspectives on the same mystery.

Human language is both a gift and a growth. It is received and developed. It is divine in origin and human in expression. And because it is human in expression, it is limited, conditioned, and shaped by the boundaries of human experience.

This chapter traces the human side of that story.

THE FIRST SYMBOLS BEFORE WORDS

Long before humans spoke in structured sentences, they communicated through symbols. Early cave paintings, handprints, and carved markings reveal a mind reaching beyond immediate survival. These symbols were not language in the modern sense, but they were the seeds of language—attempts to represent reality, memory, and meaning.

- A handprint on a cave wall is a declaration: "I was here."
- A painted animal is a memory: "This is what we hunt."
- A carved pattern is a sign: "This is our place."

These early symbols show that humans were beginning to think abstractly. They were beginning to separate the world into categories. They were beginning to represent what was not immediately present.

Symbolic thought is the soil from which language grows.

THE EMERGENCE OF SOUNDS AND SHARED MEANING

As human societies grew more complex, so did their need for communication. Sounds that were once instinctive—cries, warnings, calls—began to take on shared meaning. Over time, these sounds became intentional. They became tools for cooperation, coordination, and storytelling.

Language emerged not from solitary individuals but from communities. It was shaped by:

- the need to hunt together
- the need to warn of danger
- the need to share knowledge
- the need to teach children
- the need to remember

Language is a social invention.
It arises from relationship, not isolation.

THE BIRTH OF WORDS

Words are symbols attached to concepts. They allow humans to name the world, divide it, categorize it, and manipulate it mentally. The moment humans began naming things, they began shaping reality in their minds.

To name something is to define it.

To define it is to limit it.

To limit it is to control it.

This is the power—and the danger—of human language.

Words do not capture reality; they carve it.

Words do not reveal the whole; they reveal a part.

Words do not show the Infinite; they show the finite.

This limitation becomes crucial when humans attempt to speak about God.

GRAMMAR: THE ARCHITECTURE OF THOUGHT

As words multiplied, grammar emerged—the structure that allows humans to express relationships, actions, time, and causality. Grammar is not merely a linguistic tool; it is a cognitive architecture. It shapes how humans think.

- Subjects and objects create separation.
- Verbs create sequence.
- Tenses create time.
- Prepositions create space.
- Categories create boundaries.

Grammar is the skeleton of human thought.

It is also the boundary of human thought.

This is why human language cannot contain the Infinite.

The Infinite has no subject, no object, no sequence, no boundary.

THE EVOLUTION OF ABSTRACT THOUGHT

As language evolved, so did the human capacity for abstraction. Humans began to speak not only of things they could see, but of things they could imagine:

- justice
- beauty
- truth
- spirit
- meaning
- destiny

These abstractions allowed humans to build cultures, religions, philosophies, and civilizations. But they also introduced a new problem: *the mind began to confuse its abstractions with reality.*

Humans began to believe that their concepts were the things themselves.

They began to mistake the map for the territory.

They began to assume that their words could contain the Real.

This confusion becomes central to the later chapters of the book.

THE LIMITS OF HUMAN LANGUAGE

Human language evolved for survival, cooperation, and storytelling. It did not evolve to describe the Infinite. It is shaped by:

- the senses
- the body
- the environment
- the brain
- the social world

Language is a human tool.
It is powerful, but it is limited.
It can describe the world of experience.
It cannot contain the Source of experience.
It can name the things that exist.
It cannot name the One who gives existence.

This is why every attempt to speak about God is partial, symbolic, metaphorical, and ultimately inadequate.

THE TENSION BETWEEN DIVINE AND HUMAN LANGUAGE

Chapter 5 showed that divine language is creative, perfect, and unconditioned.

Chapter 6 shows that human language is limited, evolving, and conditioned.

This creates a tension:

- God speaks reality into being.
- Humans speak from within reality.
- God's word is generative.
- Human words are descriptive.
- God's speech is unbounded.
- Human speech is bounded.

This tension becomes the foundation for the next chapters, where we explore how humans attempt to understand the Real through the limited tools of language and thought.

THE THRESHOLD OF HUMAN LANGUAGE

To understand God, we must understand the limits of human language.

To understand the limits of human language, we must understand its origins.

And to understand its origins, we must see that language is both divine and human—a gift and a growth, a revelation and an evolution.

Human language is a window, not a wall.

It points toward the Real, but it cannot contain it.

This chapter prepares the reader for the next step:

If language is limited, *then how does the human mind understand anything at all—especially the Infinite?*

SUMMARY OF THE CHAPTER

- Human language evolved through symbols, sounds, and shared meaning.
- Words and grammar shape human thought and perception.
- Language is limited by human experience and cognition.
- Human language cannot contain the Infinite.
- Divine language is perfect; human language is conditioned.
- This tension sets the stage for the limits of human understanding.

7

HUMAN UNDERSTANDING

HUMAN BEINGS DO NOT see reality as it is. We see reality as our minds allow us to see it. Our understanding is shaped by biology, culture, memory, language, and experience. We do not perceive the world directly; we perceive it through filters. These filters help us survive, but they also limit us. They shape what we can know, what we can imagine, and what we can believe.

If language is limited (Chapters 5–6), then the mind that uses language is even more limited. Human understanding is not a clear window to the Real. It is a lens—curved, coloured, conditioned. This chapter explores the nature of that lens and reveals why the Infinite cannot be contained within it.

THE MIND AS A MEANING-MAKING MACHINE

The human mind does not passively receive information. It actively constructs meaning. It interprets, categorizes, simplifies, and organizes. It takes the overwhelming complexity of reality and reduces it to manageable patterns.

This is not a flaw. It is a survival mechanism.

- We group things into categories.
- We create stories to explain events.
- We project intentions onto others.
- We assume patterns where none exist.
- We fill gaps with imagination.

The mind is always interpreting.
It cannot stop.
It cannot see without shaping what it sees.
This means that *understanding is never pure*. It is always filtered.

THE LIMITS OF PERCEPTION

Human perception is narrow. We see only a tiny fraction of the electromagnetic spectrum. We hear only a narrow band of frequencies. We perceive only three dimensions of space. We experience time in a single direction.

Our senses are not windows to reality.

They are survival tools.

What we call "the world" is a thin slice of what exists.

What we call "understanding" is a thin slice of what the mind can process.

This limitation becomes profound when we attempt to understand the Infinite.

The Mind Creates Categories—and Then Becomes Trapped in Them

To understand anything, the mind must divide reality into categories:

- subject and object
- cause and effect
- inside and outside
- self and other
- past, present, future

These categories are not universal.

They are human.

They help us navigate the world, but they do not describe the Real.

The Real is not divided.

The Real is not sequential.

The Real is not dualistic.

The mind creates categories—and then mistakes them for reality.

This is the root of misunderstanding God.

THE PROBLEM OF PROJECTION

Human beings project their own qualities onto the world. We see intention where there is none. We see patterns where there is randomness. We see ourselves in everything.

This projection becomes dangerous when applied to God.

Humans project:

- human emotions
- human motives
- human limitations
- human forms
- human expectations

onto the Infinite.

This is how idols are born—not only physical idols, but conceptual idols.

The mind creates a God in its own image.

This projection becomes central in Chapter 9, but its roots are here.

THE MIND CANNOT GRASP THE INFINITE

The Infinite has no boundaries.

The mind understands only boundaries.
The Infinite has no form.
The mind understands only forms.
The Infinite is not an object.
The mind understands only objects.
The Infinite is not in time.
The mind understands only sequence.
The Infinite is not in space.
The mind understands only location.
The Infinite is not divided.
The mind understands only distinctions.

This is why every attempt to understand God collapses into metaphor, symbol, or silence.

THE ILLUSION OF UNDERSTANDING

Humans often believe they understand more than they do. This illusion arises because the mind simplifies reality into concepts. Concepts feel solid, but they are shadows of the Real.

- A concept is not the thing itself.
- A definition is not the reality.
- A belief is not the truth.
- A doctrine is not the Infinite.

The mind confuses its models with reality.
This confusion becomes catastrophic when applied to God.

THE COLLAPSE OF CONCEPTUAL THOUGHT

When the mind approaches the Infinite, its categories break down.
It cannot grasp what has no boundary.
It cannot imagine what has no form.
It cannot conceive what has no opposite.
This is why the mystics speak of:

- unknowing
- darkness
- silence
- emptiness
- stillness

These are not negative states.

They are the collapse of conceptual thought—the moment when the mind stops trying to grasp the Infinite and becomes open to the Real.

THE THRESHOLD OF HUMAN UNDERSTANDING

To understand God, we must first understand the limits of understanding.

To approach the Infinite, we must recognise the finitude of the mind.

To encounter the Real, we must let go of the illusion that our concepts can contain it.

Human understanding is a tool.

It is powerful, but it is limited.

It can point toward the Real, but it cannot grasp it.

This chapter prepares the reader for the next movement of the book:

If the mind is limited, how did ancient humans relate to God?

How did they understand the divine before philosophy, before abstraction, before conceptual distortion?

SUMMARY OF THE CHAPTER

- Human understanding is filtered, limited, and conditioned.
- The mind constructs meaning rather than receiving it directly.
- Perception is narrow and shaped by survival needs.

- The mind creates categories that do not apply to the Infinite.
- Humans project their own qualities onto God.
- Concepts cannot contain the Real.
- Understanding collapses at the threshold of the Infinite.

8

ANCIENT TIMES

God's Existence Was Not in Question

IN THE ANCIENT WORLD, the question "Does God exist?" did not exist. It would have made no sense to the people of early civilizations. For them, the divine was not a hypothesis, not a theory, not a belief to be defended or debated. The divine was the atmosphere of existence—the unquestioned background of life, meaning, and reality.

The modern struggle with God's existence is a recent invention. It belongs to a world shaped by skepticism, secularism, and scientific reductionism. But for most of human history, the divine was as obvious as the sun, as present as the seasons, as real as birth and death.

This chapter explores that world—a world in which God's existence was not a question, only *Who is God?*

THE ANCIENT MIND DID NOT SEPARATE THE SACRED AND THE SECULAR

Modern people divide life into categories:

- sacred and secular

- natural and supernatural
- physical and spiritual
- religious and non-religious

Ancient people did not.

For them, the world was one unified field of meaning. The divine was woven into:

- weather
- fertility
- war
- harvest
- kingship
- morality
- destiny

There was no "ordinary" world.

Everything was charged with presence.

This is why ancient cultures built temples, altars, and rituals—not to "prove" God, but to *participate* in the divine order they assumed.

MESOPOTAMIA: THE WORLD GOVERNED BY THE GODS

In ancient Mesopotamia, the earliest known civilization, the gods were not distant beings. They were the forces that shaped reality:

- Enlil, the god of wind and authority
- Enki, the god of wisdom and water
- Inanna, the goddess of love and war
- Marduk, the god of kingship and order

The question was never "Do they exist?"

The question was "Which god rules this city? Which god must we appease? Which god protects us?"

The divine was the structure of the world.

EGYPT: THE DIVINE AS COSMIC ORDER

In ancient Egypt, the divine was expressed through *ma'at*—the principle of cosmic balance, truth, and order. The gods were manifestations of this order:

- Ra, the sun
- Osiris, life and death
- Isis, motherhood
- Horus, kingship

Pharaoh was not a political leader; he was the living embodiment of divine order.

To question the gods would be to question the structure of reality itself.

Canaan and the Ancient Near East: Competing Visions of the Divine

In the lands surrounding ancient Israel, the divine world was crowded:

- Baal, the storm god
- Asherah, the mother goddess
- Molech, the god of fire
- Dagon, the grain god

These gods were not metaphors. They were the powers behind nature, fertility, and war.

The question was not "Does God exist?" but "Which god is supreme?"

This is the world into which the Hebrew Scriptures speak.

EARLY ISRAEL: THE SHIFT FROM MANY GODS TO ONE

Israel's earliest faith did not begin with philosophical monotheism. It began with a simple, relational claim:

"Our God is the true God."

The question was not "Does God exist?"

It was "Who is the true God among the gods?"

Only later did Israel's faith evolve into the radical claim:

"There is no other."

But even then, the existence of God was not debated.

It was assumed.

The debate was about identity, not existence.

GREECE: THE DIVINE AS THE STRUCTURE OF REALITY

In ancient Greece, the gods were many, but the philosophical tradition pointed toward a deeper unity:

- Plato's *Form of the Good*
- Aristotle's *Unmoved Mover*
- The Stoic *Logos*

These were not "gods" in the mythological sense.

They were metaphysical principles—the rational structure of the universe.

Even here, the divine was not questioned.

The debate was about *the nature of the divine*, not its existence.

INDIA AND CHINA: THE DIVINE AS THE GROUND OF BEING

In ancient India, the divine was expressed through *Brahman*—the Absolute, the unconditioned Real.

In ancient China, the divine was expressed through the *Tao*—the Way that underlies all things.

Neither tradition questioned the existence of the divine.

They questioned how to understand it.

WHY ANCIENT PEOPLE DID NOT DOUBT GOD

Ancient people did not doubt God because:

- the world was unpredictable
- nature was powerful
- life was fragile
- death was mysterious
- meaning was essential
- community was sacred
- ritual was central
- the divine was woven into everything

To deny the divine would be to deny the world itself.

THE MODERN QUESTION IS NOT ANCIENT

The question "Does God exist?" emerges only when:

- the world becomes disenchanted
- nature becomes mechanistic
- meaning becomes subjective
- society becomes secular
- the divine becomes optional

This is a modern condition, not an ancient one.

For ancient humanity, the divine was not a belief.

It was the *background of existence.*

THE THRESHOLD OF THE ANCIENT WORLD

Understanding the ancient world is essential for the next chapter.

If ancient people never doubted God's existence, then how did humanity drift into confusion?

How did the divine become obscured?

How did idols emerge?

How did the true God become lost in the human mind?

SUMMARY OF THE CHAPTER

- Ancient people did not question God's existence.
- The divine was woven into every aspect of life.
- Civilizations differed not on existence but on identity.
- The modern question "Does God exist?" is historically recent.
- Understanding ancient certainty prepares us to understand later confusion.

9

WHEN GOD WAS LOST IN THE MIND OF MAN

(Idolatry and Human Projections)

HUMANITY DID NOT BEGIN in confusion about God. In the ancient world, the divine was assumed, present, and woven into the fabric of life. But over time, something shifted. The clarity of the divine presence dimmed. The memory of the Real faded. The human mind, shaped by fear, desire, and imagination, began to create its own gods—gods that looked like humans, acted like humans, and served human needs.

This chapter explores that shift: how God was lost in the mind of man, and how idols emerged as substitutes for the forgotten Real.

THE DRIFT FROM REVELATION TO IMAGINATION

When the memory of the Real fades, the mind does not fall silent. It fills the void. Humans cannot live without meaning, without order, without a sense of the sacred. When the true God becomes distant, the mind creates replacements.

This drift happens slowly:

- revelation becomes tradition
- tradition becomes story
- story becomes symbol
- symbol becomes superstition
- superstition becomes fear

fear becomes control

control becomes idolatry

Idolatry is not the worship of statues.

Idolatry is the collapse of the divine into the human imagination.

THE PSYCHOLOGY OF IDOLATRY

Idolatry begins in the mind long before it appears in stone or wood. It arises from human needs:

- the need for protection
- the need for control
- the need for certainty
- the need for identity
- the need for power

When humans cannot grasp the Infinite, they shrink it into something manageable. Something visible. Something predictable. Something they can bargain with, manipulate, or appease.

Idols are not divine beings.

They are psychological projections.

They are mirrors in which humanity sees its own fears and desires reflected back.

THE BIRTH OF THE HUMAN-MADE GODS

As civilizations grew, so did their pantheons. The gods multiplied because human needs multiplied.

- Storm gods for rain
- Fertility gods for crops
- War gods for victory
- Household gods for protection
- River gods for floods
- Sun gods for life
- Death gods for the afterlife

These gods were not revelations.

They were inventions.

They were attempts to explain the unpredictable forces of nature.

They were attempts to control what could not be controlled.

The divine became fragmented into countless forms—each one a piece of the human psyche carved into myth.

NAMING THE IDOLS OF THE ANCIENT WORLD

The ancient world was filled with idols—not only physical statues, but entire systems of meaning built around human projections.

- Baal—the storm god of Canaan, feared for his power over rain and drought.
- Asherah—the mother goddess, symbol of fertility and sexuality.
- Molech—the god of fire, associated with sacrifice and fear.
- Ra—the Egyptian sun god, embodiment of cosmic order.
- Marduk—the Babylonian god of kingship and war.
- Zeus—the Greek sky god, a magnified human ruler.

- Aphrodite—the goddess of beauty and desire.
- Pan—the god of wilderness and instinct.

These gods reveal more about humanity than about the divine.

They are portraits of the human condition, not windows to the Infinite.

THE COLLAPSE OF THE DIVINE INTO THE HUMAN

Idolatry is not merely the worship of images.

It is the reduction of the Infinite to the finite.

It is the moment when:

- the divine becomes manageable
- mystery becomes myth
- transcendence becomes superstition
- the Real becomes a story
- God becomes a character
- the Infinite becomes an object

This collapse is not only ancient.

It is universal.

It is psychological.

It is ongoing.

Every time the mind tries to define God, it risks creating an idol.

THE HUMAN DESIRE FOR A VISIBLE GOD

Humans crave visibility.

We trust what we can see.

We fear what we cannot.

This is why idols are physical.

They give form to the formless.

They give shape to the shapeless.

They give presence to the invisible.

But the moment the divine is made visible, it is no longer divine.

The Infinite cannot be carved.

The Eternal cannot be shaped.

The Source cannot be contained.

Idolatry is the attempt to make the uncontainable containable.

THE LOSS OF THE REAL

When idols replace the Real, humanity loses its orientation.

The compass spins.

The sacred becomes distorted.

The divine becomes fragmented.

The mind becomes confused.

This confusion sets the stage for the later chapters of the book:

- the courtroom question "Who is God?"
- the collapse of human categories
- the impossibility of defining God

Idolatry is not a side issue.

It is the central human problem.

It is the reason the divine becomes obscured.

It is the reason the mind struggles to approach the Real.

THE THRESHOLD OF IDOLATRY

To understand God, we must understand how humanity lost God.

To understand how humanity lost God, we must understand idolatry.

To understand idolatry, we must understand the human mind.

Idolatry is not ancient history.

It is the ongoing tendency of the mind to shrink the Infinite into something it can grasp.

This chapter prepares the reader for the next movement of the book:

If humanity lost God in the mind, how did different traditions attempt to recover the Real?

How did they approach the Infinite without collapsing it into an idol?

SUMMARY OF THE CHAPTER

- Idolatry is the collapse of the divine into human imagination.
- Humans create gods in their own image.
- Ancient idols reveal human fears, desires, and projections.
- The divine becomes obscured when the Infinite is reduced to the finite.
- Idolatry is psychological, not merely physical.
- Understanding idolatry prepares us for the later chapters on the nature of God.

10

NIRVANA

AFTER HUMANITY LOST THE Real in the mind and replaced it with idols, a new question emerged across cultures: *Is there a way to approach the Infinite without collapsing it into an image?*

Most traditions answered by refining their concept of God.

Buddhism answered by removing the concept altogether.

Nirvana is not a doctrine about God.

It is a doorway into the unconditioned—a way of approaching the Real without naming it, defining it, or imagining it.

Where idolatry collapses the Infinite into the human mind, Nirvana dissolves the human mind's illusions so the Infinite can be encountered without distortion.

This chapter explores how Nirvana functions as a radical alternative to the human tendency to create gods in our own image.

THE HUMAN PROBLEM: THE ILLUSION OF A SEPARATE SELF

Buddhism begins with a diagnosis, not a theology.

It observes that suffering arises from clinging—clinging to identity, to desire, to permanence, to the illusion of a fixed self.

The self we defend, protect, and define is not a solid entity.

It is a process, a flow, a bundle of experiences held together by memory and habit.

The self is not a thing.

It is a story.

This insight is crucial.

If the self is not absolute, then the categories the self creates—including "God"—cannot be absolute either.

THE COLLAPSE OF THE CONDITIONED WORLD

Buddhism teaches that everything conditioned is impermanent.

Everything arises, changes, and dissolves.

Nothing holds itself in existence.

Nothing is independent.

Nothing is self-sustaining.

This leads to the insight of *emptiness*—not that things do not exist, but that they do not exist independently.

Everything is interdependent.

Everything is relational.

Everything is contingent.

This dissolves the idea of a separate, isolated being—whether human or divine.

NIRVANA: THE UNCONDITIONED REAL

If all conditioned things are impermanent, then the Real must be unconditioned.

This is Nirvana.

Nirvana is not a place.

It is not a heaven.

It is not annihilation.

It is not a reward.

Nirvana is the cessation of illusion.
It is the end of clinging.
It is the liberation from the false self.
It is the encounter with the Real beyond all concepts.
Nirvana is not something one "attains."
It is what remains when the illusions fall away.

THE SILENCE AROUND THE ULTIMATE

Buddhism refuses to describe Nirvana because description creates boundaries.

To describe is to define.

To define is to limit.

To limit is to distort.

This is why the Buddha remained silent on metaphysical questions:

- Is the universe eternal?
- Is the soul permanent?
- Does God exist?
- What is the nature of the Absolute?

This silence is not avoidance.

It is precision.

The Buddha understood that any answer would trap the Infinite inside a concept.

Silence protects the Real from distortion.

THE FLAME AND THE WIND

One of the oldest metaphors for Nirvana is the extinguishing of a flame.

Not the destruction of the flame—the release of the flame.

A flame goes out not because it dies, but because the conditions that sustained it have ceased.

The flame returns to its source.
This is Nirvana:
the end of the conditions that sustain illusion.
Another metaphor is the wind.
You cannot see the wind, but you see its effects.
You cannot grasp the wind, but you feel its presence.
You cannot define the wind, but you know it is real.
Nirvana is like this—real, present, ungraspable.

THE INFINITE WITHOUT GOD-LANGUAGE

Nirvana is the clearest example in world philosophy of approaching the Infinite without using the word "God."

It shows:

- the Real does not require a name
- the Infinite does not require a form
- transcendence does not require a deity
- liberation does not require belief

This does not deny the divine.
It purifies the approach to the divine.
Nirvana removes the last human projections.
It strips away the final anthropomorphic images.
It reveals the Infinite as unconditioned, unbounded, and beyond all categories.

This prepares the reader for the next chapter, where the distinction between the finite and the Infinite becomes explicit.

THE THRESHOLD OF NIRVANA

To understand God, we must understand the human mind's tendency to create idols.

To understand Nirvana, we must understand the mind's capacity to dissolve them.

Nirvana is not a doctrine to be accepted.
It is a mirror held up to the mind.
It shows that:

- the self is not absolute
- concepts are not reality
- language cannot contain the Infinite
- the Real is encountered through letting go, not grasping

Nirvana is the final purification before the ascent into the Infinite.

SUMMARY OF THE CHAPTER

- Buddhism approaches the Infinite without God-language.
- The self is an illusion; clinging creates suffering.
- All conditioned things are impermanent and empty.
- Nirvana is the unconditioned Real beyond all concepts.
- Silence protects the Infinite from distortion.
- Nirvana purifies the mind of projections and prepares it for the Infinite.

11

THE FINITE AND THE INFINITE

HUMAN BEINGS LIVE WITHIN limits. We think in limits, speak in limits, imagine in limits, and understand in limits. Everything we know is shaped by boundaries—beginnings and endings, here and there, before and after, cause and effect. These limits are not flaws; they are the conditions of human existence. But they create a profound problem when we attempt to approach the Infinite.

The Infinite has no boundaries.

The human mind cannot think without them.

This chapter explores the absolute difference between the finite and the Infinite—a difference so vast that it exposes why every human attempt to define God collapses before it begins.

THE FINITE MIND AND ITS BOUNDARIES

The human mind is structured by limitation. It understands by dividing, categorizing, comparing, and contrasting. It cannot grasp anything without placing it inside a mental frame.

The mind requires:

- form
- sequence
- location
- identity
- distinction
- boundary

These are the tools of human understanding.

They are also the walls of human understanding.

The mind cannot think outside these categories because it is built from them.

THE INFINITE HAS NO BOUNDARIES

The Infinite is not simply "very large."

It is not an extension of the finite.

It is not a quantity.

The Infinite is *boundlessness.*

It has:

- no edges
- no form
- no beginning
- no end
- no division
- no opposite

The Infinite is not one thing among many.

It is not even "one" in the numerical sense.

It is the ground from which all things arise.

This is why the Infinite cannot be imagined.

Imagination requires form.

The Infinite has none.

THE COLLAPSE OF HUMAN CATEGORIES

When the finite mind tries to grasp the Infinite, its categories break down.

- *Form collapses because the Infinite has no shape.*
- *Time collapses because the Infinite has no sequence.*
- *Space collapses because the Infinite has no location.*
- *Identity collapses because the Infinite has no boundaries.*
- *Comparison collapses because the Infinite has no opposite.*

The mind reaches for the Infinite and finds nothing it can hold.

Not because the Infinite is absent, but because the mind is too small.

This collapse is not failure.

It is revelation.

THE INFINITE CANNOT BE DIVIDED

The finite world is full of divisions:

- light and dark
- good and evil
- self and other
- sacred and profane
- being and non-being

These divisions belong to the human mind, not to the Infinite.
The Infinite cannot be split.
It cannot be compared.
It cannot be placed alongside anything else.
To divide the Infinite is to misunderstand it.
To compare the Infinite is to reduce it.
To define the Infinite is to destroy it.

THE INFINITE CANNOT BE CONTAINED IN THOUGHT

Thought is finite.

It moves in sequence.

It uses symbols.

It relies on memory.

It operates through contrast.

The Infinite is not sequential.

It is not symbolic.

It is not remembered.

It is not contrasted.

Thought cannot contain the Infinite because the Infinite is not an object of thought.

It is the ground of thought.

This is why the mystics speak of:

- unknowing
- silence
- darkness
- stillness
- surrender

These are not poetic metaphors.

They are descriptions of what happens when the finite mind approaches the Infinite.

The Infinite Cannot Be Defined

To define something is to place boundaries around it.

To say what it is and what it is not.

To limit it.

But the Infinite has no boundaries.

It cannot be placed inside a definition.

It cannot be captured in a concept.

It cannot be reduced to a doctrine.

This is why every definition of God fails.

Not because God is vague, but because God is Infinite.

Definition belongs to the finite.
Transcendence belongs to the Infinite.

THE HUMAN TENDENCY TO SHRINK THE INFINITE

Faced with the Infinite, the human mind instinctively shrinks it into something manageable:

- a being
- a person
- a force
- a ruler
- a judge
- a father
- a king

These images are not wrong.
They are incomplete.
They are attempts to translate the Infinite into finite categories.
But every translation distorts.
Every image reduces.
Every concept collapses.
This is the root of idolatry—not statues, but concepts.

THE THRESHOLD OF THE INFINITE

To understand God, we must understand the Infinite.
To understand the Infinite, we must understand the finite.
And to understand the finite, we must understand its limits.
The finite cannot grasp the Infinite.
But it can be opened by it.

SUMMARY OF THE CHAPTER

- The human mind is finite and structured by boundaries.
- The Infinite has no boundaries and cannot be divided.
- Human categories collapse when applied to the Infinite.
- Thought cannot contain the Infinite because thought is finite.
- Every definition of God fails because definition requires limits.
- The mind shrinks the Infinite into images it can grasp.
- Understanding the Infinite prepares the reader for the limits of faith and philosophy.

12

FAITH AND PHILOSOPHY

HUMANITY HAS ALWAYS REACHED toward the Infinite. Across cultures and centuries, two great pathways emerged: *faith and philosophy*. One trusts. The other questions. One receives. The other seeks. One begins with revelation. The other begins with reason. These two paths have shaped civilizations, scriptures, doctrines, and entire worldviews.

But both paths share a limitation:

They are human attempts to approach the Infinite using finite tools.

This chapter explores how faith and philosophy each rise toward the Real—and why both ultimately fall silent before the Infinite.

FAITH: TRUST IN THE REAL

Faith begins with encounter.

It begins with the sense that the world is not empty, that life is not accidental, that meaning is not invented. Faith is the human response to the presence of the Real—a presence felt before it is understood.

Faith is not belief in doctrines.

Faith is trust in the Real.

Faith says:

- the Infinite is personal
- the Infinite is relational
- the Infinite speaks
- the Infinite reveals
- the Infinite calls

Faith is the human answer to divine initiative.

But faith has limits.

It expresses the Infinite through stories, symbols, rituals, and metaphors.

These are powerful, but they are also human.

They translate the Infinite into forms the mind can grasp.

Faith points toward the Real.

But it cannot contain it.

PHILOSOPHY: INQUIRY INTO THE REAL

Philosophy begins not with encounter but with questioning.

It asks:

- What is ultimate reality?
- What is the ground of being?
- What is the nature of truth?
- What is the structure of existence?

Philosophy seeks clarity.

It seeks coherence.

It seeks understanding.

Through logic, reflection, and metaphysical reasoning, philosophy rises toward the Infinite.

It strips away illusions.

It exposes contradictions.

It dissolves false images of God.

But philosophy has limits.

It uses concepts, and concepts are finite.

It uses language, and language is bounded.

It uses thought, and thought cannot grasp the Infinite.

Philosophy points toward the Real.

But it cannot reach it.

THE STRENGTHS AND LIMITS OF FAITH

Faith can see what reason cannot.

It can trust what the mind cannot prove.

It can receive what the intellect cannot grasp.

Faith is powerful because:

- it opens the heart
- it awakens intuition
- it creates relationship
- it transcends logic
- it embraces mystery

But faith can also distort.

It can cling to images.

It can absolutize metaphors.

It can confuse symbol with reality.

It can turn revelation into dogma.

It can turn trust into certainty.

Faith can rise toward the Infinite —

but it can also create idols.

THE STRENGTHS AND LIMITS OF PHILOSOPHY

Philosophy can see what faith sometimes ignores.

It can question assumptions.
It can expose contradictions.
It can refine concepts.
It can purify language.
Philosophy is powerful because:

- it seeks truth
- it demands clarity
- it challenges illusion
- it dismantles false gods
- it reveals the limits of thought

But philosophy can also distort.
It can reduce the Infinite to an idea.
It can confuse abstraction with reality.
It can mistake analysis for encounter.
It can turn mystery into argument.
Philosophy can rise toward the Infinite —
but it can also collapse into speculation.

THE MEETING POINT OF FAITH AND PHILOSOPHY

At their best, faith and philosophy do not oppose each other.

They complete each other.
Faith without philosophy becomes superstition.
Philosophy without faith becomes abstraction.
Faith gives philosophy direction.
Philosophy gives faith clarity.
Both rise toward the Real.
Both purify the mind.
Both expose illusions.
Both point beyond themselves.

And both ultimately fall silent before the Infinite.

THE COLLAPSE OF BOTH PATHS AT THE THRESHOLD

When faith reaches the Infinite, it becomes awe.

When philosophy reaches the Infinite, it becomes silence.

Faith cannot define the Infinite.

Philosophy cannot conceptualize the Infinite.

Both paths end where the Infinite begins.

This is not failure.

It is revelation.

The Infinite is not reached by belief or by logic.

It is encountered when the mind's categories collapse.

This collapse prepares the reader for the courtroom chapters—where the question "Who is God?" is placed on trial, and where the limits of faith and philosophy become the very evidence for the transcendence of the Real.

THE THRESHOLD OF FAITH AND PHILOSOPHY

To understand God, we must understand the limits of our approaches to God.

Faith rises through trust.

Philosophy rises through inquiry.

Both rise toward the Real.

Both fall short.

SUMMARY OF THE CHAPTER

- Faith and philosophy are the two great human approaches to the Infinite.
- Faith trusts; philosophy questions.

- Both rise toward the Real but remain limited by human categories.
- Faith can create idols; philosophy can reduce the Infinite to abstraction.
- Both paths collapse at the threshold of the Infinite.
- This collapse prepares the reader for the courtroom chapters.

13

WHO IS GOD?

The One in Question

For thousands of years, humanity has spoken about God. We have prayed, argued, worshipped, doubted, defined, defended, and denied. We have built temples and doctrines, philosophies and rituals, idols and ideas. But beneath all of this lies a single, ancient, unrelenting question—a question older than religion, older than philosophy, older than language itself:

Who is God?

This question is not simple.

It is not innocent.

It is not neutral.

It is a question that exposes the limits of the human mind, the boundaries of language, and the illusions of the self. It is a question that cannot be answered without first revealing the one who asks it.

This chapter opens the courtroom—not a courtroom of law, but a courtroom of meaning—where the question of God is placed on trial.

THE QUESTION THAT CANNOT BE AVOIDED

Every culture has asked this question.

Every civilization has shaped its identity around it.

Every human being, at some point, confronts it.

The question "Who is God?" is not merely theological.

It is existential.

It asks:

- What is the source of reality?
- What is the ground of being?
- What is the meaning of existence?
- What is the origin of consciousness?
- What is the foundation of morality?
- What is the purpose of life?

To ask "Who is God?" is to ask what lies behind everything.

This is why the question cannot be avoided.

It is the question behind all questions.

THE PROBLEM OF THE QUESTIONER

Before we can ask who God is, we must ask who *we* are.

The question "Who is God?" is shaped by the mind that asks it.

And as we have seen:

- the mind is finite
- the mind is conditioned
- the mind is limited
- the mind is shaped by language
- the mind is shaped by culture
- the mind is shaped by fear and desire

A finite mind cannot grasp the Infinite.

A conditioned mind cannot comprehend the Unconditioned.

This means the question "Who is God?" is already compromised.

It is already distorted.

It is already too small.

The courtroom opens with a paradox:

The one asking the question is not capable of understanding the answer.

THE COLLAPSE OF THE OLD IMAGES

Humanity has filled the world with images of God:

- king
- judge
- warrior
- father
- mother
- creator
- ruler
- protector

These images are not wrong.

They are incomplete.

They are metaphors—attempts to translate the Infinite into human categories.

But every metaphor collapses under its own weight.

A king is limited.

A judge is partial.

A warrior is violent.

A father is human.

A creator is separate from creation.

The Infinite cannot be contained in any of these images.

The courtroom begins by clearing the room of idols—not statues, but concepts.

THE COURTROOM OF MEANING

In this courtroom, there are no witnesses.

There is no jury.

There is no prosecution or defense.

There is only the question and the silence that surrounds it.

The courtroom is the human mind.

The judge is the Infinite.

The evidence is existence itself.

The question "Who is God?" is placed before the Real—not to be answered, but to be revealed.

This courtroom is not about proving God.

It is about exposing the limits of the question.

THE BURDEN OF PROOF

In human courts, the burden of proof lies on the one making the claim.

But in the courtroom of meaning, the burden of proof lies on the question itself.

The question must prove that it is capable of being asked.

It must prove that it is coherent.

It must prove that it is meaningful.

But how can a finite question contain an Infinite answer?

How can a bounded mind grasp an unbounded reality?

How can language describe what lies beyond language?

The courtroom reveals that the question "Who is God?" is too small for the Infinite.

THE INFINITE AS THE ONE IN QUESTION

The Infinite is not on trial.

The question is.

The Infinite does not need to defend itself.

The Infinite does not need to explain itself.

The Infinite does not need to justify itself.

The question "Who is God?" is the one being examined.
Is it a valid question?
Is it a coherent question?
Is it even possible?

THE THRESHOLD OF THE COURTROOM

To understand God, we must first understand the question.

To understand the question, we must understand the mind that asks it.

To understand the mind, we must understand its limits.

SUMMARY OF THE CHAPTER

- The question "Who is God?" is ancient, universal, and unavoidable.
- The question is shaped by the finite, conditioned human mind.
- Human images of God are metaphors, not definitions.
- The courtroom of meaning examines the question, not the Infinite.
- The burden of proof lies on the question itself.
- This chapter opens the trial; the next chapter presents the first argument.

14

GOD AS THE GROUND OF BEING

THE QUESTION HAS BEEN placed before the Infinite: *Who is God?*

But before any answer can be approached, the old framework must be dismantled. The question "Who is God?" assumes that God is a being—a supreme being, perhaps, but still a being among beings. This assumption is the first illusion that must fall.

God is not a being.

God is the *Ground of Being*—the source, the foundation, the condition that makes all existence possible.

This chapter reveals the first major argument of the courtroom:

If God exists, God does not exist *as things exist.*

God is the reason anything exists at all.

THE ERROR OF THINKING OF GOD AS A BEING

Human language forces us to think in categories.

Everything we know is a "thing"—an object, an entity, a form.

So when we speak of God, we instinctively imagine:

- a powerful being
- a cosmic ruler
- a divine person
- a heavenly king
- a supernatural entity

These images are natural.

They are also false.

A being is limited.

A being is located.

A being is defined.

A being is one among many.

But the Infinite cannot be limited, located, defined, or compared.

The Infinite cannot be "one" in the numerical sense.

To call God "a being"—even the greatest being—is to shrink the Infinite into the finite.

BEING ITSELF VS. A BEING

There is a difference between *a being and Being itself.*

- A being *has* existence.
- Being itself *is* existence.

A being depends on something else for its existence.

Being itself depends on nothing.

A being is conditioned.

Being itself is unconditioned.

A being is finite.

Being itself is Infinite.

God is not a being who exists.

God is the *source of existence.*

This is why the courtroom must shift the question from:

"Does God exist?"

to

"What is the source of existence?"
The first question is too small.
The second question opens the door to the Infinite.

THE GROUND BENEATH ALL THINGS

Everything that exists depends on something else:

- a tree depends on soil
- soil depends on earth
- earth depends on gravity
- gravity depends on physical laws
- physical laws depend on the structure of reality

Every chain of explanation leads deeper.
Every cause leads to another cause.
Every foundation rests on another foundation.
But the chain cannot be infinite.

There must be a ground—a reality that does not depend on anything else.

This ground cannot be a thing.
It cannot be an object.
It cannot be a being.

It must be the *Ground of Being*—the unconditioned source from which all conditioned things arise.

This is what the word "God" points to.

THE INFINITE AS THE SOURCE, NOT AN OBJECT

If God is the Ground of Being, then God is not an object in the universe.

God is not even an object outside the universe.
God is not *in* the universe.
The universe is *in* God.
God is not a part of reality.

Reality is a manifestation of God.

God is not a being who exists.

God is the *reason existence is possible.*

This is why the courtroom must reject the old question "Where is God?"

The Infinite cannot be located.

Location belongs to the finite.

God is not somewhere.

God is the *condition for somewhere.*

THE COLLAPSE OF THE SPATIAL IMAGINATION

When people imagine God, they imagine:

- above
- beyond
- outside
- elsewhere

These are spatial metaphors.

They belong to the human mind, not to the Infinite.

The Infinite is not "up there."

The Infinite is not "out there."

The Infinite is not "beyond the universe."

The Infinite is the *ground beneath* the universe—the depth, not the distance.

God is not far.

God is foundational.

THE COLLAPSE OF THE TEMPORAL IMAGINATION

People also imagine God as:

- before creation
- after the end

- acting in time
- responding in time

But time is a condition of the finite.

The Infinite is not in time.

Time is in the Infinite.

God does not "wait."

God does not "begin."

God does not "end."

God is the *ground of time*, not a participant in it.

This is why the courtroom must reject the question "When did God begin?"

The Infinite has no beginning.

Beginnings belong to the finite.

THE INFINITE AS THE NECESSARY REALITY

Everything that exists is contingent—it could have been otherwise.

But the Ground of Being is necessary—it cannot not be.

If the Ground of Being did not exist, nothing would exist.

Not matter.

Not energy.

Not space.

Not time.

Not consciousness.

Not possibility.

The Ground of Being is the condition for all conditions.

The foundation for all foundations.

The reality behind all realities.

This is what the courtroom must recognize:

God is not an answer within the universe.

God is the reason there is a universe.

THE THRESHOLD OF THE GROUND OF BEING

To understand God, we must stop thinking of God as a being.

To understand the Infinite, we must stop thinking in finite categories.

To understand the Ground of Being, we must let go of the images that limit it.

This chapter presents the first major argument of the courtroom:

God is not a being who exists.

God is the *Ground of Being*—the Infinite source from which all existence flows.

SUMMARY OF THE CHAPTER

- God is not a being; God is the Ground of Being.
- A being is finite and conditioned; the Infinite is unconditioned.
- God is the source of existence, not an object within existence.
- The universe is in God, not the other way around.
- Spatial and temporal metaphors collapse when applied to the Infinite.
- The Ground of Being is necessary; all other things are contingent.
- This chapter presents the first courtroom argument; the next chapter presents the second.

15

THE IMPOSSIBILITY OF DEFINING GOD

THE COURTROOM HAS HEARD the first argument:

God is not a being among beings, but the Ground of Being itself.

Now the second argument must be examined—the argument that no human definition of God is possible. Not because God is vague, but because definition itself is a tool of the finite mind, and the Infinite cannot be placed inside a finite frame.

This chapter reveals the verdict:

God cannot be defined.

Not partially.

Not metaphorically.

Not conceptually.

Not philosophically.

Not theologically.

The impossibility of defining God is not a failure of language.

It is a revelation of transcendence.

THE NATURE OF DEFINITION

To define something is to place boundaries around it.

A definition says:

- what something is
- what something is not
- where it begins
- where it ends
- how it differs from other things

Definition is a tool of the finite mind.
It works only on finite things.
A tree can be defined.
A river can be defined.
A planet can be defined.
A concept can be defined.
But the Infinite has no boundaries.
It has no edges.
It has no opposite.
It has no outside.
Definition collapses at the threshold of the Infinite.

EVERY DEFINITION REDUCES GOD

When humans define God, they reduce the Infinite to something manageable:

- "God is love."
- "God is power."
- "God is creator."
- "God is judge."
- "God is father."
- "God is king."

These statements are not wrong.

They are incomplete.

They are metaphors—attempts to translate the Infinite into human categories.

But every metaphor shrinks the Real.

Every definition becomes an idol.

The moment God is defined, God is diminished.

THE LIMITS OF LANGUAGE

Language is built from distinctions:

- subject and object
- noun and verb
- cause and effect
- here and there
- before and after

These distinctions do not apply to the Infinite.

Language cannot speak without dividing.

The Infinite cannot be divided.

Language cannot describe without limiting.

The Infinite cannot be limited.

Language cannot name without separating.

The Infinite cannot be separated.

This is why the courtroom must acknowledge that language is too small for the Infinite.

THE LIMITS OF THOUGHT

Thought operates through concepts.

Concepts operate through boundaries.

Boundaries operate through exclusion.

To think is to divide.

To define is to limit.

To conceptualize is to reduce.

But the Infinite has no divisions.

The Infinite has no limits.

The Infinite cannot be reduced.

Thought cannot grasp the Infinite because thought is finite.

This is why the mystics speak of unknowing—not ignorance, but the collapse of conceptual thought at the threshold of the Real.

THE LIMITS OF IMAGINATION

Imagination creates images.

Images require form.

Form requires boundaries.

But the Infinite has no form.

The Infinite cannot be pictured.

The Infinite cannot be visualized.

Every image of God is a human projection.

Every projection is an idol.

Every idol is a distortion.

The courtroom must reject imagination as a tool for defining the Infinite.

THE LIMITS OF DOCTRINE

Doctrines are structured definitions.

They attempt to describe the nature of God in precise terms.

But doctrines are:

- linguistic
- conceptual
- cultural
- historical
- finite

Doctrines can point toward the Real.

But they cannot contain it.
The Infinite cannot be captured in a creed.
The Infinite cannot be confined to a system.
The Infinite cannot be reduced to a statement.
Doctrine is a map, not the territory.
A symbol, not the Real.

THE COLLAPSE OF ALL HUMAN CATEGORIES

When the courtroom examines the question "Who is God?" it discovers that:

- language collapses
- thought collapses
- imagination collapses
- doctrine collapses
- definition collapses

Not because God is absent, but because the Infinite exceeds every human category.

The courtroom does not declare God unknowable.
It declares God *undefinable.*
There is a difference.
The Infinite can be encountered.
The Infinite can be known in experience.
The Infinite can be recognized in being.
But the Infinite cannot be defined.

THE VERDICT OF THE COURTROOM

The courtroom delivers its verdict:

The question "Who is God?" cannot be answered through definition.

The Infinite cannot be contained in a finite concept.

God is not an object to be described, but the Ground of Being itself.

This is not the end of understanding.

It is the beginning.

When definition collapses, encounter becomes possible.

When concepts fall silent, the Real can be seen.

When the mind stops grasping, the Infinite becomes present.

The courtroom does not close with certainty.

It closes with clarity.

THE THRESHOLD BEYOND DEFINITION

To understand God, we must let go of the need to define God.

To approach the Infinite, we must release the tools of the finite.

To encounter the Real, we must step beyond language, thought, and image.

SUMMARY

- Definition requires boundaries; the Infinite has none.
- Every definition of God reduces the Infinite to the finite.
- Language, thought, imagination, and doctrine cannot contain the Real.
- All human categories collapse at the threshold of the Infinite.
- The courtroom's verdict: God cannot be defined.
- This collapse is not failure but revelation—the opening to encounter.

16

WHEN THE MIND FALLS SILENT

THE QUESTION "WHO IS God?" has collapsed under its own weight.

Language has reached its limit.

Thought has reached its boundary.

Definition has dissolved.

What remains is silence—not the silence of absence, but the silence of presence.

Not the silence of ignorance, but the silence of clarity.

Not the silence of emptiness, but the silence of fullness.

This chapter explores what happens when the mind falls silent and the Infinite is no longer approached through concepts, but encountered through being.

THE END OF THE CONCEPTUAL PATH

The human mind has exhausted its tools:

- language
- definition
- doctrine

- imagination
- philosophy
- theology

Each tool rose toward the Infinite.
Each tool collapsed at the threshold.
The collapse is not a failure.
It is the necessary end of the conceptual path.
The mind cannot grasp the Infinite.
But it can be opened by it.

When the mind falls silent, the Real becomes visible—not as an object, but as the ground of all experience.

THE SILENCE THAT REVEALS

There are two kinds of silence:

- the silence of not knowing
- the silence of knowing too deeply for words

The first is ignorance.
The second is revelation.

The silence that follows the collapse of definition is the second kind.

It is the silence that arises when the mind recognizes its limits and stops trying to grasp what cannot be grasped.

This silence is not empty.
It is luminous.
It reveals:

- the presence beneath thought
- the being beneath identity
- the ground beneath existence
- the Real beneath all appearances

This is the silence in which the Infinite is encountered.

THE PRESENCE BENEATH ALL THINGS

When the mind falls silent, something becomes clear:

The Infinite is not far.
The Infinite is not hidden.
The Infinite is not elsewhere.
The Infinite is the presence beneath all things.
It is the ground of:

- awareness
- existence
- consciousness
- being

It is not an object in experience.
It is the condition for experience.
It is not something the mind can see.
It is the reason the mind can see at all.
This presence is not reached through effort.
It is revealed when effort ceases.

THE COLLAPSE OF THE SEPARATE SELF

When the mind falls silent, the illusion of the separate self begins to dissolve.

The self is seen not as a fixed entity, but as a pattern—a story, a movement, a process.

The boundaries that once felt solid begin to soften:

- the boundary between self and world
- the boundary between inner and outer
- the boundary between sacred and ordinary
- the boundary between human and divine

These boundaries were never real.
They were constructs of the mind.

When the mind falls silent, the boundaries fall with it.
What remains is unity—not as a concept, but as a lived reality.

THE REAL IS NOT FOUND—IT IS REVEALED

The Infinite is not discovered.
It is uncovered.
It is not reached.
It is recognized.
It is not attained.
It is revealed.
The Real is not something added to experience.
It is what remains when illusion is removed.
This is why the mystics speak of awakening, not acquisition.
The Infinite is not something gained.
It is something seen.

THE END OF SEEKING

Seeking is the movement of the mind.
It is the attempt to grasp, to understand, to define, to control.
But the Infinite cannot be sought.
It can only be encountered.
Seeking ends when the seeker dissolves.
The mind falls silent.
The boundaries fall away.
The Real stands revealed.
This is the end of the courtroom.
Not a verdict, but a vision.

THE THRESHOLD OF SILENCE

To understand God, the mind must fall silent.
To encounter the Infinite, the self must loosen.
To see the Real, the boundaries must dissolve.

This chapter marks the end of the conceptual journey and the beginning of the existential one.

SUMMARY OF THE CHAPTER

- The collapse of definition leads to silence, not emptiness.
- This silence is the space where the Infinite is encountered.
- The Real is not grasped by thought but revealed in being.
- The separate self dissolves when the mind falls silent.
- Seeking ends, and recognition begins.
- This chapter ends the courtroom sequence and opens the path to transformation.

17

THE RETURN TO SEEING

When the mind falls silent, something subtle begins to shift. The world does not change, but the way we see it does. The self does not disappear, but the way we relate to it dissolves. The Infinite does not arrive, because it was never absent—but the veil that concealed it begins to lift.

This chapter explores what happens after the collapse of definition, after the courtroom falls quiet, after the mind stops grasping. It is the beginning of a new kind of seeing—not conceptual, not imaginative, not doctrinal, but direct.

THE WORLD AFTER SILENCE

When the mind stops trying to define the Real, the Real begins to reveal itself.

Not as an object.
Not as a concept.
Not as a belief.
But as presence.

The world appears the same—trees, sky, faces, movement—yet everything feels different.

The edges soften.

The boundaries loosen.

The sense of separation begins to fade.

The world is no longer a collection of objects.

It is a field of being.

This is the first sign of the return to seeing.

THE SELF AFTER SILENCE

The self does not vanish.

It becomes transparent.

The old identity—the defended, anxious, grasping self—begins to feel like a costume.

A role.

A habit.

The self is still present, but it is no longer the center.

It is no longer the reference point.

It is no longer the boundary between "me" and "the world."

The self becomes a movement within being, not a separate entity.

This is the second sign of the return to seeing.

The Presence Beneath Experience

When the mind falls silent, a deeper presence becomes noticeable—not as a thought, not as a feeling, but as the ground of experience itself.

This presence is:

- steady
- quiet
- unchanging
- intimate
- vast

It is not something added to experience.

It is what experience arises from.

It is not something the mind can grasp.

It is what allows the mind to grasp anything at all.

This presence is the Infinite, not as a concept, but as the ground of being.

THE COLLAPSE OF THE OLD DIVISIONS

As seeing deepens, the old divisions begin to dissolve:

- inner vs. outer
- sacred vs. ordinary
- spiritual vs. physical
- self vs. world
- God vs. creation

These divisions were never real.

They were constructs of the finite mind.

When the mind falls silent, the constructs fall with it.

What remains is unity—not as an idea, but as a lived perception.

This unity is not mystical.

It is natural.

It is the way reality has always been.

THE RETURN OF MEANING

Meaning does not disappear when definitions collapse.

It becomes deeper.

Meaning is no longer something imposed on the world.

It is something revealed by the world.

Meaning is not created by thought.

It is perceived by awareness.

Meaning is not a story.

It is a presence.

This is why the return to seeing feels like remembering something ancient—something known before language, before doctrine, before identity.

THE REAL IS NOT ELSEWHERE

The Infinite is not found in distant realms.

It is not hidden behind the world.

It is not waiting in some future state.

The Infinite is here.

In this moment.

In this breath.

In this awareness.

The Real is not elsewhere.

It is the depth of everything.

This is the heart of the return to seeing:

The Infinite is not beyond the world.

The Infinite is within the world—as its ground, its presence, its being.

THE END OF THE SEARCH

When the mind falls silent, the search ends.

Not because the answer has been found, but because the question dissolves.

The seeker disappears.

The seeking disappears.

What remains is being.

The Infinite is not reached.

It is recognized.

This recognition is not dramatic.

It is quiet.

It is simple.

It is clear.

It is the return to seeing.

SUMMARY

- After silence, a new kind of seeing emerges.
- The world appears as a field of being, not a collection of objects.
- The self becomes transparent and no longer central.
- A deeper presence becomes noticeable beneath all experience.
- Old divisions dissolve, revealing unity.
- Meaning returns as presence, not concept.
- The search ends, and recognition begins.
- This chapter begins the transformation that follows the collapse of definition.

18

THE SHIFT IN BEING

When the mind returns to seeing, something deeper begins to unfold.

Seeing changes perception.

But being changes existence.

This chapter explores the transformation that occurs when the Infinite is no longer approached through thought, but lived through presence. It is not a change in belief, nor a change in doctrine, nor a change in philosophy. It is a change in the structure of experience itself—a shift in how one stands in the world.

This shift is subtle, but decisive.

Quiet, but irreversible.

It does not announce itself.

It reveals itself.

THE REORIENTATION OF THE INNER LIFE

When the Infinite becomes present, the inner life reorganizes itself.

The old center—the anxious, defended, grasping self—begins to dissolve.

A new center emerges, not as an identity, but as a depth.
This depth is:

- steady
- quiet
- spacious
- unthreatened
- unhurried

The inner life no longer revolves around fear or desire.
It revolves around presence.
This presence is not something one holds.
It is something one rests in.
The Softening of the Ego
The ego does not disappear.
It loses its throne.
The ego becomes a tool, not a master.
A function, not an identity.
A movement, not a boundary.
The ego still speaks, but it no longer dictates.
It still reacts, but it no longer defines.
It still appears, but it no longer claims ownership.
This softening is not self-denial.
It is self-clarity.
The ego is seen for what it is:
a temporary pattern within the field of being.

THE TRANSFORMATION OF ACTION

When being shifts, action shifts with it.
Action is no longer driven by:

- fear
- insecurity
- comparison

- ambition
- approval
- avoidance

Action arises from clarity, not compulsion.
From presence, not pressure.
From understanding, not reaction.
This does not make action passive.
It makes action precise.
The mind no longer acts to defend the self.
It acts to express the Real.

THE TRANSFORMATION OF RELATIONSHIP

When the boundaries of the self soften, the boundaries between selves soften as well.

Relationship becomes less about negotiation and more about recognition.

Others are no longer seen as:

- threats
- competitors
- instruments
- obstacles
- mirrors for the ego

They are seen as expressions of the same ground of being.
This recognition does not erase difference.
It reveals unity beneath difference.
Relationship becomes a meeting of presence with presence.

THE TRANSFORMATION OF PERCEPTION

The world is no longer a collection of separate objects.

It is a single field of being expressing itself in countless forms.

Perception becomes:

- quieter
- clearer
- less reactive
- more spacious
- more intimate

The world is not "out there."

It is within the same presence that perceives it.

This is not a mystical vision.

It is the natural perception that arises when the mind stops dividing reality into fragments.

THE END OF RESISTANCE

Resistance is the ego's attempt to control reality.

It manifests as tension, fear, avoidance, and struggle.

When being shifts, resistance dissolves.

Not because everything becomes easy, but because the self no longer stands apart from reality.

Life is no longer something to fight.

It is something to participate in.

This does not create passivity.

It creates alignment.

Action becomes fluid.

Response becomes natural.

Life becomes coherent.

THE EMERGENCE OF STILLNESS

Stillness is not the absence of movement.

It is the absence of inner conflict.

Stillness is the natural state of being when the mind is no longer divided against itself.

It is the quiet beneath thought.
The depth beneath emotion.
The presence beneath identity.
This stillness is not something one achieves.
It is something one uncovers.
It was always there.
The noise was covering it.

THE INFINITE AS LIVED REALITY

The Infinite is no longer a concept.
It is the ground of experience.
It is not something one believes in.
It is something one lives from.
This shift is not dramatic.
It is subtle.
It is steady.
It is transformative.
It changes how one sees, acts, relates, and exists.
This is the shift in being.

SUMMARY

- After seeing, being begins to shift.
- The inner life reorganizes around presence, not ego.
- Action becomes clear, precise, and unforced.
- Relationship becomes recognition, not negotiation.
- Perception becomes unified and spacious.
- Resistance dissolves, and stillness emerges.
- The Infinite becomes a lived reality, not a concept.
- This chapter begins the integration of the transformation.

19

THE DEEPENING OF A NEW LIFE

When the shift in being begins, it does not remain a moment.

It becomes a movement.

It begins quietly, almost imperceptibly, but it continues to unfold long after the initial recognition.

The Infinite, once glimpsed, does not recede.

It begins to permeate the structure of life.

This chapter explores how the transformation that began in silence and presence deepens over time—how it stabilizes, matures, and becomes the foundation of a new way of living.

THE SLOW STABILIZATION OF PRESENCE

Presence is not a state one enters and leaves.

It is the ground that becomes more and more familiar.

At first, presence appears in moments—brief openings, flashes of clarity, intervals of stillness.

But over time, these moments lengthen.

They begin to overlap.

They become the background of experience.

Presence becomes:

- the default orientation
- the quiet center
- the steady ground
- the unshakable depth

This stabilization is not dramatic.
It is subtle, like dawn slowly brightening a landscape.

THE DISSOLVING OF OLD PATTERNS

As presence stabilizes, old patterns begin to dissolve.
Not through effort, but through irrelevance.
Patterns built on fear lose their power.
Patterns built on desire lose their urgency.
Patterns built on identity lose their authority.
The mind no longer reacts from habit.
It responds from clarity.
This dissolution is not forced.
It is natural.
Illusions cannot survive in the light of presence.

THE EMERGENCE OF INNER COHERENCE

A new coherence begins to form—not imposed, but discovered.
Life begins to align with itself.
Contradictions soften.
Conflicts resolve.
The inner world becomes less divided.
This coherence is not perfection.
It is integration.
The self is no longer split between:

- what it fears and what it desires
- what it shows and what it hides

- what it believes and what it doubts

The self becomes whole—not by becoming more, but by becoming less divided.

THE TRANSFORMATION OF TIME

When presence deepens, time changes.

Not externally, but internally.

The mind no longer lives in:

- anticipation
- memory
- projection
- regret
- expectation

The present moment becomes the center of gravity.

Not as a discipline, but as a natural orientation.

Time becomes spacious.

Events unfold without pressure.

Life is lived, not chased.

This transformation is not about mindfulness.

It is about being.

THE TRANSFORMATION OF SUFFERING

Suffering does not disappear.

But its nature changes.

Pain still arises.

Loss still occurs.

Challenges still appear.

But suffering—the psychological resistance to what is—begins to dissolve.

Suffering is no longer amplified by:

- identification
- fear
- narrative
- resistance

Pain is felt directly, without the added weight of the ego's story.
This makes suffering lighter, clearer, and more bearable.
This is not detachment.
It is freedom.

THE EMERGENCE OF COMPASSION

As the boundaries of the self soften, compassion deepens.
Not as a moral duty, but as a natural expression of unity.
Compassion arises because:

- others are no longer separate
- suffering is recognized as universal
- presence sees presence
- being recognizes being

Compassion becomes effortless.
It becomes the natural response of a heart no longer defended.
This compassion is not sentimental.
It is grounded, clear, and steady.

THE RETURN TO ORDINARY LIFE

The deepening of being does not remove one from the world.
It returns one to the world more fully.
Ordinary life becomes:

- simpler
- clearer
- more intimate

- more meaningful

  Tasks are no longer burdens.
  Relationships are no longer negotiations.
  Moments are no longer stepping stones to somewhere else.
  Life becomes enough.
  Not because it has changed, but because the one living it has.

THE INFINITE IN DAILY LIFE

The Infinite is no longer a concept or an experience.
It becomes the quiet background of every moment.
It is present:

- in breath
- in movement
- in conversation
- in silence
- in work
- in rest

The Infinite is not something one visits.
It is something one lives from.
This is the deepening of a new life.

SUMMARY OF THE CHAPTER

- Presence stabilizes slowly and becomes the ground of experience.
- Old patterns dissolve naturally in the light of clarity.
- Inner coherence emerges as the self becomes less divided.
- Time becomes spacious and centered in the present.
- Suffering transforms as resistance dissolves.

- Compassion arises naturally from unity.
- Ordinary life becomes intimate and meaningful.
- The Infinite becomes the background of daily existence.
- This chapter marks the deepening of transformation and the beginning of maturity.

20

THE LONG ARC OF TRANSFORMATION

TRANSFORMATION DOES NOT END with insight.

It does not end with silence.

It does not end with presence.

It begins there.

The shift in being that once felt subtle becomes the axis around which life turns.

The Infinite, once glimpsed, becomes the ground from which one lives.

This chapter explores the long arc of transformation—the slow, steady unfolding of a life aligned with the Real.

This arc is not dramatic.

It is deep.

It is not sudden.

It is enduring.

It is not mystical.

It is human.

THE SLOW RIPENING OF AWARENESS

Awareness matures the way fruit ripens—gradually, naturally, without force.

What begins as moments of clarity becomes a continuous field.

What begins as glimpses becomes vision.

What begins as presence becomes identity.

This ripening is marked by:

- increasing steadiness
- decreasing reactivity
- deeper clarity
- quieter mind
- softer ego
- wider compassion

Awareness becomes less like a state and more like a climate—the atmosphere in which life unfolds.

THE REWRITING OF THE INNER NARRATIVE

The old narrative—the story of the separate self—begins to dissolve.

Not through rejection, but through irrelevance.

The story loses its authority.

Its urgency fades.

Its grip loosens.

A new narrative emerges, not constructed but discovered:]

- life as unfolding
- self as expression
- being as primary
- presence as home

This new narrative is not about identity.

It is about alignment.

THE REORIENTATION OF PURPOSE

Purpose is no longer something one invents.

It is something one uncovers.

Purpose arises from:

- clarity
- presence
- compassion
- alignment
- understanding

It is not driven by ambition.

It is guided by coherence.

Purpose becomes less about achieving and more about expressing—expressing the Real through action, relationship, and being.

This purpose is not chosen.

It is lived.

THE TRANSFORMATION OF DESIRE

Desire does not disappear.

It becomes transparent.

Desire is no longer a demand.

It is a movement.

It no longer defines identity.

It no longer dictates action.

It no longer creates suffering.

Desire becomes:

- lighter
- clearer

- less compulsive
- more aligned

Desire is no longer the master.
It becomes a signal—a whisper of direction, not a command.

THE DEEPENING OF COMPASSION

Compassion matures into something steady and unforced.

It is no longer reactive.

It is responsive.

Compassion arises because the boundaries of the self have softened.

The suffering of others is no longer "their" suffering.

It is the suffering of being itself.

This compassion is not sentimental.

It is grounded.

It is clear.

It is strong.

It does not collapse into pity.

It does not avoid pain.

It meets reality as it is.

THE EMERGENCE OF WISDOM

Wisdom is not knowledge.

It is clarity of being.

Wisdom arises when:

- the mind is quiet
- the ego is soft
- presence is steady
- perception is clear

Wisdom is the ability to see without distortion.
To act without compulsion.

To respond without fear.
Wisdom is not something one acquires.
It is something one becomes.

THE INTEGRATION OF THE INFINITE AND THE ORDINARY

The Infinite does not remove one from the world.

It deepens one's participation in it.

The ordinary becomes luminous:

- washing dishes
- walking
- speaking
- listening
- resting
- working

The Infinite is not found in extraordinary experiences.

It is found in the depth of ordinary life.

This integration is the hallmark of maturity—the realization that the Real is not elsewhere, but here.

THE QUIET CONFIDENCE OF BEING

A quiet confidence emerges—not arrogance, not certainty, but groundedness.

This confidence comes from:

- knowing the self is not separate
- knowing the Real is present
- knowing life unfolds from being
- knowing fear no longer defines action

This confidence is not loud.

It is steady.
It does not need to prove.
It does not need to defend.
It does not need to grasp.
It simply is.

THE LONG ARC AS A RETURN

The long arc of transformation is not a journey toward something new.

It is a return to something ancient—the ground of being that was always present.

The arc bends toward:

- simplicity
- clarity
- presence
- compassion
- wisdom
- unity

This is not the end of the journey.
It is the beginning of a life lived from the Real.

SUMMARY

- Transformation matures slowly and steadily.
- Awareness ripens into a continuous field.
- The old narrative dissolves; a new coherence emerges.
- Purpose becomes expression, not ambition.
- Desire becomes transparent and aligned.
- Compassion deepens into clarity and strength.

- Wisdom arises from presence, not knowledge.
- The Infinite becomes integrated into ordinary life.
- A quiet confidence emerges from alignment with the Real.
- This chapter marks the long arc of transformation and the threshold of fulfillment.

21

THE RETURN TO THE WORLD

Every transformation eventually returns to the world.

Not to escape it, not to transcend it, but to inhabit it more fully.

The journey inward—through silence, presence, and the collapse of the old self—does not end in isolation.

It ends in participation.

This chapter explores the return to the world after the long arc of transformation.

It is the moment where the Infinite becomes embodied in action, relationship, and ordinary life.

It is not a withdrawal from humanity, but a deeper entry into it.

THE WORLD AS IT ALWAYS WAS

The world does not change.

The mind changes.

And because the mind changes, the world appears different.

The same streets, the same faces, the same responsibilities, the same routines—yet everything feels more spacious, more intimate, more alive.

The world is no longer a field of objects.

It is a field of being.

This is the first sign of the return:

The world is seen as it always was, not as the mind once imagined it.

THE SELF AS A FUNCTION, NOT AN IDENTITY

The self returns, but not as the center.

It returns as a tool—a way of navigating the world, not a boundary that separates one from it.

The self becomes:

- lighter
- more flexible
- less defended
- less reactive
- more transparent

Identity is no longer a prison.

It is a garment—worn lightly, removed easily, never mistaken for the body beneath.

This allows one to move through the world without the weight of selfconcern.

THE RETURN OF RESPONSIBILITY

Transformation does not remove responsibility.

It deepens it.

Responsibility is no longer driven by fear, guilt, or obligation.

It arises from clarity.

One acts because action is needed.

One speaks because speech is appropriate.

One helps because suffering is recognized.

One creates because creation is natural.

Responsibility becomes an expression of being, not a burden placed upon it.

THE RETURN OF RELATIONSHIP

Relationship becomes the arena where transformation is tested, expressed, and embodied.

Others are no longer mirrors for the ego.

They are expressions of the same ground of being.

This changes everything:

- conflict becomes communication
- misunderstanding becomes curiosity
- difference becomes richness
- connection becomes natural
- compassion becomes instinctive

Relationship is no longer a negotiation of needs.

It is a meeting of presence with presence.

THE RETURN OF WORK

Work does not disappear.

It becomes aligned.

Work is no longer a means of selfvalidation.

It is an expression of clarity.

Work becomes:

- simpler
- more focused
- less anxious
- more meaningful

The quality of work changes because the one doing the work has changed.

Work becomes a form of presence—a way of participating in the unfolding of the world.

THE RETURN OF CREATIVITY

Creativity deepens when the mind is no longer divided.

It becomes less about expression of the self and more about expression of the Real.

Creativity becomes:

- fluid
- intuitive
- unforced
- spacious
- authentic

The creative act is no longer an attempt to prove something.

It is a way of revealing something.

The Infinite expresses itself through form—through art, writing, movement, speech, and silence.

THE RETURN OF DIFFICULTY

Transformation does not remove difficulty.

It changes the relationship to it.

Challenges still arise.

Loss still occurs.

Pain still appears.

But difficulty is no longer interpreted as failure.

It is seen as part of the unfolding of being.

Difficulty becomes:

- a teacher
- a mirror
- a threshold
- a refinement

The mind no longer collapses under difficulty.
It meets difficulty with presence.

THE RETURN OF JOY

Joy returns—not as excitement, not as pleasure, not as achievement, but as a quiet, steady undercurrent.

Joy arises from:

- alignment
- clarity
- presence
- unity
- being

This joy is not dependent on circumstances.
It is the natural fragrance of a life lived from the Real.

THE RETURN WITHOUT THE OLD BURDEN

The return to the world is not a return to the old life.

It is a return without the old burden:

- without the burden of identity
- without the burden of fear
- without the burden of seeking
- without the burden of becoming
- without the burden of separation

One returns to the world as one who is no longer separate from it.

This is the essence of the return.

SUMMARY

- Transformation returns one to the world, not away from it.
- The world is seen as a field of being, not a field of objects.
- The self becomes a function, not an identity.
- Responsibility arises from clarity, not obligation.
- Relationship becomes presence meeting presence.
- Work becomes aligned and meaningful.
- Creativity becomes an expression of the Real.
- Difficulty becomes a teacher, not a threat.
- Joy becomes a steady undercurrent of being.
- This chapter marks the beginning of embodiment and the return to the world.

22

THE UNITY OF GOD, SELF, AND REALITY

THE JOURNEY THAT BEGAN with questions, concepts, idols, and definitions now arrives at a deeper clarity.

The courtroom has fallen silent.

The mind has returned to seeing.

Being has shifted.

Life has deepened.

The world has been reentered with new eyes.

Now the threads begin to converge.

This chapter explores the unity that emerges when the Infinite is no longer approached as an object, but recognized as the ground of God, the ground of self, and the ground of reality.

This unity is not a doctrine.

It is not a belief.

It is not a philosophy.

It is a recognition.

THE THREE GREAT QUESTIONS

Every human life is shaped by three questions:

- Who is God?
- Who am I?
- What is reality?

These questions appear separate.
They are not.
They are three faces of the same inquiry.
Three windows into the same depth.

- Three movements toward the same ground.

When the Infinite becomes present, the separation between these questions dissolves.

GOD AS THE GROUND OF BEING

The courtroom revealed that God is not a being among beings.

God is the *Ground of Being*—the unconditioned source from which all existence arises.

This means:

- God is not separate from reality.
- God is not separate from the self.
- God is the depth of both.

God is not an object in the universe.
God is the reason the universe is possible.
This recognition dissolves the old images and reveals the Infinite as the ground of all things.

THE SELF AS EXPRESSION OF BEING

When the self is seen clearly, it is no longer a separate entity.

It is a movement within being—a temporary expression of the Infinite.

The self is:

- not independent
- not isolated
- not absolute
- not separate

The self is a wave in the ocean of being.

It rises, moves, dissolves—but it is never apart from the water.

This recognition dissolves the illusion of separation.

REALITY AS THE FIELD OF BEING

Reality is not a collection of objects.

It is a field of being—a continuous expression of the Infinite in form.

Every form is temporary.

Every form is dependent.

Every form is interconnected.

Reality is not "out there."

It is the unfolding of the same ground that appears as the self.

This recognition dissolves the boundary between inner and outer.

THE CONVERGENCE OF THE THREE

When God is understood as the Ground of Being,
and the self is understood as an expression of being,
and reality is understood as the field of being,
a profound unity emerges:
God, self, and reality are not three separate domains.
They are three dimensions of the same Infinite ground.
This is not pantheism.

It is not monism.
It is not mysticism.
It is the recognition that the Infinite is the depth of all things.

THE END OF SEPARATION

Separation was always an illusion—a necessary illusion for the finite mind, but an illusion nonetheless.

The mind divided reality into:

- God and world
- self and other
- sacred and ordinary
- inner and outer
- spiritual and physical

These divisions collapse when the Infinite is recognized as the ground of all.

There is no "God over there" and "self over here."
There is no "sacred realm" and "ordinary realm."
There is no "spiritual world" and "physical world."
There is only being—expressing itself in countless forms.

THE UNITY THAT DOES NOT ERASE DIFFERENCE

Unity does not erase individuality.

It reveals the depth beneath it.
A wave is not the ocean,
but it is never separate from it.
A leaf is not the tree,
but it is never separate from it.
A person is not the Infinite,
but they are never separate from it.
Unity is not sameness.

Unity is shared ground.

THE INFINITE AS THE HEART OF ALL THINGS

When the Infinite is recognized as the ground of God, self, and reality, everything becomes transparent to its source.

The Infinite is:

- the depth of consciousness
- the ground of existence
- the presence beneath experience
- the being within all beings

This recognition is not conceptual.

It is existential.

It is the moment where the journey inward becomes the journey outward—where the Infinite is seen in all things.

THE INTEGRATION OF THE JOURNEY

The journey of this book—from idolatry to silence, from collapse to clarity, from separation to unity—now converges into a single understanding:

The Infinite is the ground of God, the ground of the self, and the ground of reality.

To know one is to know all.

This is the unity that emerges when the mind falls silent and being becomes clear.

THE THRESHOLD OF COMPLETION

This chapter marks the beginning of the final movement—the integration of the entire journey into a coherent vision of existence.

The next chapter will explore the implications of this unity—how it reshapes understanding, meaning, and the human relationship to the Real.

SUMMARY

- The three great questions—God, self, reality—converge into one.
- God is the Ground of Being, not a separate being.
- The self is an expression of being, not an isolated entity.
- Reality is the field of being, not a collection of objects.
- Unity emerges when the Infinite is recognized as the ground of all.
- Separation dissolves, but individuality remains as expression.
- This chapter integrates the journey and prepares for the final movement.

23

THE VISION OF THE REAL

When unity is recognized—when God, self, and reality are seen as expressions of the same Infinite ground—a new vision begins to form.

Not a mystical vision.

Not a philosophical system.

Not a religious doctrine.

A vision of the Real.

This chapter explores the clarity that emerges when the Infinite is no longer a concept but the living ground of existence.

It is the moment where the entire journey—from idolatry to silence, from collapse to presence, from separation to unity—becomes a single, coherent understanding.

THE REAL BEYOND ALL IMAGES

The Real is not an image.

It is not a form.

It is not a concept.

It is not a belief.

The Real is the ground beneath all images, forms, concepts, and beliefs.

The mind once tried to imagine God.
Now it sees that God cannot be imagined.
The mind once tried to define God.
Now it sees that God cannot be defined.
The mind once tried to locate God.
Now it sees that God cannot be located.
The Real is not something the mind grasps.
It is what the mind arises from.

THE REAL AS PRESENCE

Presence is the first taste of the Real.

Not presence as a state, but presence as the ground of experience.

Presence is:

- silent
- steady
- unchanging
- intimate
- infinite

Presence is not something one enters.
It is something one recognizes.
It is the depth beneath thought, emotion, and perception.
It is the Infinite appearing as awareness.
This presence is the Real.

THE REAL AS BEING

Being is the second taste of the Real.

Not being as existence of objects, but being as the foundation of all existence.

Being is:

- unconditioned
- indivisible
- boundless
- eternal
- foundational

Being is not something that exists.
It is the reason anything exists.
This being is the Real.

THE REAL AS UNITY

Unity is the third taste of the Real.
Not unity as sameness, but unity as shared ground.
Unity does not erase difference.
It reveals the depth beneath difference.
Unity is:

- the ground of God
- the ground of self
- the ground of reality

Unity is not a belief.
It is a recognition.
This unity is the Real.

THE REAL AS THE GROUND OF GOD

God is no longer imagined as a being.
God is recognized as the Infinite ground of being.
God is:

- not separate
- not distant

- not elsewhere
- not an object

God is the depth of existence itself.
This is not a reduction of God.
It is the unveiling of God.
The Real is the ground of God.

THE REAL AS THE GROUND OF THE SELF

The self is no longer imagined as an isolated entity.
It is recognized as a movement within being.
The self is:

- temporary
- relational
- transparent
- expressive

The self is not the center of reality.
It is an expression of reality.
The Real is the ground of the self.

THE REAL AS THE GROUND OF REALITY

Reality is no longer imagined as a collection of separate objects.
It is recognized as a continuous field of being.
Reality is:

- interconnected
- interdependent
- unified
- expressive

Reality is not outside the self.
It is the same ground appearing in form.

The Real is the ground of reality.

THE VISION THAT EMERGES

When the Real is recognized as the ground of God, self, and reality, a new vision emerges—a vision that is not conceptual but existential.

This vision sees:

- God in the depth of being
- the self as expression of being
- the world as manifestation of being
- the Infinite as the ground of all

This vision is not mystical.
It is natural.
It is the way reality has always been.
The mind simply sees it now.

THE END OF THE OLD QUESTIONS

The old questions dissolve:

- "Where is God?"
- "Who am I?"
- "What is real?"

These questions belonged to the mind that believed in separation.

When unity is recognized, the questions fall away.

Not because they are answered, but because they are no longer needed.

The Real is selfevident.

THE BEGINNING OF A NEW UNDERSTANDING

This chapter marks the beginning of a new understanding—not intellectual, but existential.

Not conceptual, but lived.

Not theoretical, but real.

The next chapter will explore how this vision reshapes the meaning of life, death, purpose, and the human journey.

SUMMARY

- The Real is the ground beneath all images and concepts.
- Presence, being, and unity are three dimensions of the Real.
- God is the Infinite ground of being, not a separate being.
- The self is an expression of being, not an isolated entity.
- Reality is a field of being, not a collection of objects.
- All three converge into a single vision of the Real.
- The old questions dissolve as unity becomes clear.
- This chapter marks the beginning of a new understanding of existence.

24

THE MEANING OF LIFE AND DEATH IN THE LIGHT OF THE REAL

When the Real is recognized as the ground of God, self, and reality, the great human questions begin to shift.

Life is no longer a journey toward something missing.

Death is no longer a threat to something separate.

Purpose is no longer a project of the ego.

Meaning is no longer something constructed.

This chapter explores how the unified vision of the Real transforms the deepest human concerns—not by answering them, but by revealing their true nature.

LIFE AS EXPRESSION OF THE REAL

Life is no longer seen as a personal possession.

It is an expression of being—a movement of the Infinite appearing in form.

Life is:

- temporary in form
- eternal in ground
- individual in expression
- unified in essence

Life is not something the self "has."
Life is what the self *is*—a wave rising from the ocean of being.
This recognition dissolves the fear of living incorrectly.
Life unfolds from being, not from effort.

DEATH AS TRANSFORMATION, NOT ANNIHILATION

Death is no longer the opposite of life.
It is the transformation of form within the same ground.
A wave does not die when it falls.
It returns to the ocean.
A leaf does not vanish when it drops.
It returns to the soil.
A person does not cease when the body dissolves.
They return to the ground of being from which they arose.
Death is not the end of being.
It is the end of a particular expression of being.
This recognition dissolves the fear of death.
Death becomes a threshold, not a termination.

PURPOSE AS ALIGNMENT, NOT ACHIEVEMENT

Purpose is no longer a goal to be reached.
It is a way of being.
Purpose arises naturally when life aligns with the Real.
It is not chosen by the ego.
It is revealed by presence.
Purpose becomes:

- expression rather than ambition
- clarity rather than striving
- coherence rather than control
- participation rather than possession

Purpose is not something one invents.
It is something one embodies.

MEANING AS PRESENCE, NOT CONSTRUCTION

Meaning is no longer something the mind creates.

It is something the heart perceives.

Meaning arises from:

- unity
- presence
- clarity
- compassion
- being

Meaning is not a story.
It is a depth.
Meaning is not a belief.
It is a recognition.
Meaning is not an answer.
It is a way of seeing.

SUFFERING IN THE LIGHT OF THE REAL

Suffering does not disappear.

But its nature changes.

Suffering is no longer interpreted as punishment, failure, or cosmic injustice.

It is seen as part of the unfolding of being—a movement within the same ground that gives rise to joy, clarity, and presence.

Suffering becomes:

- a teacher
- a threshold
- a refinement
- a deepening

Suffering is no longer amplified by the ego's story.
It is met with presence, not resistance.
This transforms suffering without denying it.

LOVE AS RECOGNITION OF SHARED BEING

Love deepens when unity is recognized.
Love is no longer attachment, possession, or desire.
It is recognition.
Love is the recognition that:

- the other is not separate
- the same ground lives in both
- compassion is natural
- connection is inherent

Love becomes the natural expression of unity.
It is not something one tries to feel.
It is something one sees.

DESTINY AS UNFOLDING, NOT CONTROL

Destiny is no longer imagined as a fixed path or predetermined plan.
It is the unfolding of being through form.
Destiny is:

- not imposed
- not scripted

- not predetermined

Destiny is the natural movement of life when it is aligned with the Real.

The ego does not control destiny.

It participates in it.

Destiny is not fate.

It is coherence.

THE HUMAN JOURNEY REINTERPRETED

The human journey is no longer a climb toward the divine.

It is the recognition that the divine was the ground all along.

The journey is:

- from illusion to clarity
- from separation to unity
- from fear to presence
- from identity to being
- from seeking to recognition

The journey does not end in transcendence.

It ends in intimacy—with life, with self, with reality, with the Infinite.

THE REAL AS THE MEANING OF EXISTENCE

When the Real is recognized, the meaning of existence becomes clear:

Existence is the Infinite expressing itself in form.

Life is the Infinite appearing as a person.

Death is the Infinite returning to itself.

Purpose is the Infinite expressing through action.

Love is the Infinite recognizing itself in another.

Meaning is not added to life.

Meaning is the nature of life.

The Threshold Before the Final Movement

This chapter marks the threshold before the final movement of the book—the closing synthesis, where the entire journey is gathered into a single, coherent vision of God, self, and reality.

The next chapter will bring the book toward its culmination—the final clarity that the Infinite is not something to be reached, but something that has always been the ground of everything.

SUMMARY

- Life is an expression of the Real, not a possession of the self.
- Death is transformation, not annihilation.
- Purpose arises from alignment, not ambition.
- Meaning is presence, not construction.
- Suffering becomes a teacher when met with clarity.
- Love becomes recognition of shared being.
- Destiny becomes unfolding, not control.
- The human journey is the movement from illusion to recognition.
- The Real becomes the meaning of existence.

25

THE CLARITY BEYOND ALL SEEKING

When the Real is recognized as the ground of God, self, and reality, something profound becomes clear: the entire journey—the questions, the searching, the collapse, the silence, the transformation—was never about reaching something distant. It was about uncovering what was always present.

This chapter explores the clarity that emerges when seeking ends, when the mind rests, and when the Infinite is recognized not as a destination, but as the ground of every moment.

THE END OF THE SEARCH

Seeking is the movement of the mind toward something it believes is missing.

But when the Infinite is recognized as the ground of being, nothing is missing.

The search ends not because all questions are answered, but because the one who asked them dissolves into clarity.

Seeking ends when:

- the mind stops grasping
- the self stops defending
- the heart stops fearing
- the Real becomes evident

The end of seeking is not resignation.
It is recognition.

THE REAL WAS ALWAYS HERE

The Infinite was never elsewhere.
It was never hidden.
It was never distant.
It was concealed only by:

- the mind's concepts
- the ego's boundaries
- the self's narratives
- the fear of letting go

When these fall away, the Real stands revealed—not as something new, but as something ancient, intimate, and everpresent.
The Real is not discovered.
It is uncovered.

THE SIMPLICITY OF THE REAL

The Real is not complex.
It is simple—so simple the mind overlooks it.
The Real is:

- the presence in awareness
- the being in existence

- the unity beneath difference
- the depth within experience

The mind seeks complexity.
The Real is simplicity itself.
This simplicity is not shallow.
It is profound.

THE TRANSPARENCY OF THE WORLD

When clarity deepens, the world becomes transparent to its source.
Objects are still objects.
People are still people.
Life is still life.
But everything is seen through the lens of being.
The world is no longer opaque.
It is luminous.
The Real shines through:

- every form
- every moment
- every breath
- every encounter

The world becomes a window, not a wall.

THE TRANSPARENCY OF THE SELF

The self becomes transparent as well.
It is no longer a barrier.
It is no longer a boundary.
It is no longer a separate entity.
The self is seen as:

- a movement
- a pattern

- a wave
- an expression

The self is not denied.
It is understood.
This understanding frees the self from the burden of being the center of reality.

THE TRANSPARENCY OF GOD

God becomes transparent too—not in the sense of disappearing, but in the sense of being recognized as the depth of all things.

God is no longer imagined as:

- a distant ruler
- a cosmic judge
- a separate being

God is recognized as:

- the ground of being
- the presence in awareness
- the Infinite expressing itself in form

God is not elsewhere.
God is the depth of here.

THE CLARITY THAT REMAINS

When seeking ends, clarity remains.
This clarity is not intellectual.
It is existential.
Clarity is:

- the recognition of unity
- the dissolution of separation

- the transparency of self and world
- the presence of the Infinite in all things

Clarity is not a state.
It is the nature of the Real.

THE FREEDOM OF BEING

Freedom arises when the self is no longer bound by illusion.
This freedom is not the freedom to do anything.
It is the freedom from the need to be anything.
Freedom is:

- the absence of inner conflict
- the end of resistance
- the dissolution of fear
- the alignment with being

Freedom is not achieved.
It is revealed.

THE PEACE THAT CANNOT BE SHAKEN

Peace emerges when the mind rests in the Real.
This peace is not the absence of difficulty.
It is the absence of division.
Peace is:

- steady
- quiet
- deep
- unshakable

It does not depend on circumstances.
It arises from the ground of being itself.
This peace is the fragrance of clarity.

SUMMARY

- Seeking ends when the Real is recognized as everpresent.
- The Infinite was never distant; it was concealed by the mind's illusions.
- The Real is simple, transparent, and intimate.
- The world becomes luminous when seen through the lens of being.
- The self becomes transparent and unburdened.
- God is recognized as the depth of all things.
- Clarity, freedom, and peace arise naturally from recognition.
- This chapter marks the culmination of the ascent and prepares for the final movement.

26

THE WHOLE THAT WAS ALWAYS THERE

When clarity settles and the Real becomes evident, something remarkable happens: the entire journey rearranges itself in memory. What once felt like a sequence of steps—questions, collapses, revelations, transformations—is now seen as a single movement. A whole. A unity.

This chapter explores the recognition that the journey was never a path toward the Real, but a path through the illusions that concealed it. The Real was always present. The whole was always there.

THE JOURNEY REINTERPRETED

Looking back from clarity, the journey appears different.

What once felt like progress now feels like unveiling.

What once felt like seeking now feels like remembering.

The stages of the journey—idolatry, collapse, silence, presence, unity—are no longer separate chapters.

They are facets of a single process: the dissolution of illusion.
The journey was not linear.
It was circular.
It returned to what was always true.

THE REAL AS THE CONSTANT

Throughout the entire journey, one thing never changed: the Real.

The Real was present:

- before the questions
- during the confusion
- beneath the idols
- behind the definitions
- within the silence
- throughout the transformation

The Real did not appear at the end.
It was recognized at the end.
The Real was the constant.
The journey was the variable.

THE MIND AS THE VEIL

The mind was not the enemy.

It was the veil.

The mind created:

- images of God
- stories of self
- boundaries of reality
- fears of death
- illusions of separation

These were not mistakes.

They were developmental necessities—the scaffolding through which consciousness grows.

But once the scaffolding is no longer needed, it falls away.

The mind does not disappear.

It becomes transparent.

THE SELF AS A TEMPORARY EXPRESSION

The self, once believed to be the center of existence, is now seen as a temporary expression of being—a wave in the ocean of the Real.

The self is:

- finite in form
- infinite in ground
- unique in expression
- unified in essence

The self was never separate.

It only appeared separate.

This recognition dissolves the existential tension that once defined human life.

GOD AS THE DEPTH OF ALL THINGS

God is no longer imagined as a distant being.

God is recognized as the depth of all things—the Infinite ground of being itself.

God is:

- not elsewhere
- not later
- not beyond
- not above

God is the depth of here.
The depth of now.
The depth of being.
This recognition unifies theology, philosophy, and experience.

REALITY AS THE EXPRESSION OF THE REAL

Reality is no longer a collection of separate objects.

It is the continuous expression of the Real in form.

Reality is:

- dynamic
- interconnected
- unified
- alive

The world is not a stage on which life happens.

It is the unfolding of being itself.

This recognition dissolves the boundary between the sacred and the ordinary.

THE WHOLE THAT EMERGES

When God, self, and reality are seen as expressions of the same ground, a profound unity emerges—not as a belief, but as a recognition.

The whole is:

- simple
- coherent
- luminous
- inevitable

This whole was always present.

The journey was the process of seeing it.

THE END OF FRAGMENTATION

Fragmentation was the mind's interpretation of reality.

Unity is reality itself.

Fragmentation created:

- conflict
- fear
- confusion
- suffering

Unity reveals:

- peace
- clarity
- coherence
- compassion

The end of fragmentation is the beginning of wisdom.

THE REAL AS THE FINAL CONTEXT

Everything that once seemed separate—life, death, purpose, suffering, love—now appears within a single context: the Real.

The Real is:

- the ground of existence
- the depth of consciousness
- the unity of all things
- the meaning of life

This is the whole that was always there.

SUMMARY

- The journey is reinterpreted as a single movement of unveiling.
- The Real was always present; the journey revealed it.
- The mind was the veil, not the enemy.
- The self is a temporary expression of being.
- God is the depth of all things, not a separate being.
- Reality is the expression of the Real in form.
- Unity replaces fragmentation.
- The Real becomes the final context for all understanding.
- This chapter prepares for the final synthesis.

27

THE FINAL SYNTHESIS

The Real as All in All

WHEN THE JOURNEY IS seen as a single movement, when the mind becomes transparent, when the self loosens, when the Infinite becomes present, a final clarity emerges—not as a conclusion, but as a recognition.

This clarity is simple, luminous, and unavoidable:

The Real is all in all.

This chapter gathers the entire book into one coherent vision—the vision that arises when God, self, and reality are understood from the ground of being.

THE REAL AS THE ONLY GROUND

Everything that exists shares a single ground.

This ground is not a thing.

It is not an object.

It is not a being.

It is:

- unconditioned
- infinite
- indivisible
- foundational

This ground is what the word "God" points toward when freed from images, definitions, and projections.

God is not a being who exists.

God is the *ground of existence.*

This is the first pillar of the final synthesis.

THE SELF AS A MOVEMENT OF THE REAL

The self is not separate from the Real.

It is a temporary expression of it—a wave rising from the ocean of being.

The self is:

- finite in form
- infinite in ground
- unique in expression
- unified in essence

The self is not the center of reality.

It is a manifestation of reality.

This is the second pillar of the final synthesis.

REALITY AS THE EXPRESSION OF THE REAL

Reality is not a collection of separate objects.

It is the continuous unfolding of the Real in form.

Reality is:

- interconnected
- interdependent

- dynamic
- alive

The world is not outside the Infinite.
It is the Infinite appearing as the world.
This is the third pillar of the final synthesis.

THE COLLAPSE OF SEPARATION

When these three pillars are seen together—God as ground, self as expression, reality as manifestation—the illusion of separation dissolves.

There is no "God over there" and "self over here."
There is no "spiritual realm" and "physical realm."
There is no "inner world" and "outer world."
There is only the Real, appearing in countless forms.
Separation was a misunderstanding of perspective.
Unity is the truth of being.

THE REAL AS THE HEART OF ALL EXPERIENCE

The Real is not distant.
It is intimate.
It is:

- the presence in awareness
- the being in existence
- the depth in perception
- the silence beneath thought

The Real is not something one reaches.
It is what one always is.
This recognition is the end of seeking.

THE REAL AS THE MEANING OF GOD

When the Infinite is recognized as the ground of being, the meaning of "God" becomes clear:

God is not a character.
God is not an object.
God is not a concept.
God is:

- the depth of existence
- the source of being
- the unity of all things
- the presence within awareness

God is not separate from reality.
God is the Real.

THE REAL AS THE MEANING OF SELF

When the self is recognized as a movement of being, identity becomes transparent.

The self is:

- not isolated
- not absolute
- not permanent

The self is a form through which the Real expresses itself.
This dissolves fear, softens ego, and reveals compassion.

THE REAL AS THE MEANING OF REALITY

When reality is recognized as the expression of the Infinite, the world becomes luminous.

The world is:

- sacred
- unified
- alive
- meaningful

The Real is not behind the world.
It is within the world.
The world is the Real in form.

THE REAL AS THE MEANING OF LIFE

Life is not a journey toward the divine.
Life is the divine unfolding as a human being.
Life is:

- expression
- participation
- revelation
- presence

Life is not something one controls.
It is something one embodies.

THE REAL AS THE MEANING OF DEATH

Death is not the end of being.
It is the end of a particular expression of being.
Death is:

- transformation
- return
- dissolution of form
- continuity of ground

Nothing real is lost.

Only form changes.

THE REAL AS THE MEANING OF EVERYTHING

When the Real is recognized as all in all, everything becomes transparent to its source.

Meaning is no longer constructed.
Meaning is revealed.
Purpose is no longer invented.
Purpose is expressed.
Love is no longer attachment.
Love is recognition.
Wisdom is no longer knowledge.
Wisdom is clarity.
Peace is no longer circumstantial.
Peace is the nature of being.
This is the final synthesis.

THE THRESHOLD BEFORE THE CLOSING MOVEMENT

This chapter gathers the entire journey into a single vision:

The Real is the ground of God, the ground of the self, and the ground of reality.

To see this is to see everything.

SUMMARY

- The Real is the unconditioned ground of all existence.
- God is the depth of being, not a separate being.
- The self is a temporary expression of the Real.
- Reality is the manifestation of the Real in form.
- Separation dissolves; unity becomes evident.

- The Real becomes the meaning of God, self, world, life, and death.
- This chapter completes the final synthesis and prepares for the closing movement.

28

LIVING FROM THE REAL

When the final synthesis becomes clear—when the Real is recognized as the ground of God, the ground of the self, and the ground of reality—the question that remains is simple and profound:

How does one live from this clarity?

This chapter explores the descent from recognition into embodiment—the movement where the Infinite becomes the foundation of daily life, not as an idea but as a lived reality.

THE DESCENT AFTER THE ASCENT

Every ascent must be followed by a descent.

The summit is not a place to remain.

It is a place to see clearly.

The descent is the return to:

- ordinary moments
- ordinary tasks
- ordinary relationships

- ordinary responsibilities

But nothing is ordinary anymore.
The descent is not a fall from clarity.
It is the expression of clarity.

LIVING WITHOUT THE OLD CENTER

The old center—the defended, anxious, grasping self—no longer holds the axis of life.

A new center emerges, not as an identity but as a depth.
This depth is:

- quiet
- steady
- unshaken
- unhurried

Life is no longer lived from fear or desire.
It is lived from being.
This does not remove challenges.
It removes the illusion that challenges define the self.

ACTION WITHOUT COMPULSION

Action arises naturally when the Real is the ground.

It is no longer driven by:

- insecurity
- comparison
- ambition
- avoidance
- selfprotection

Action becomes:

- precise
- clear
- appropriate
- unforced

The body moves.

The mind thinks.

The heart responds.

But none of it is driven by the old compulsion to become something.

Action becomes expression, not escape.

SPEECH THAT EMERGES FROM CLARITY

Speech changes when the Real becomes the ground.

Words are no longer used to defend identity or manipulate outcomes.

Speech becomes:

- simple
- honest
- direct
- compassionate

Silence becomes comfortable.

Words arise only when needed.

Communication becomes a meeting of presence with presence.

Speech becomes a bridge, not a weapon.

RELATIONSHIP WITHOUT FEAR

Relationship transforms when the illusion of separation dissolves.

Others are no longer threats or instruments.

They are expressions of the same ground.

Relationship becomes:

- less reactive
- more open
- more patient
- more intimate

Conflict does not disappear.

But it loses its existential weight.

Relationship becomes a space where the Real recognizes itself in another form.

WORK AS PARTICIPATION, NOT PERFORMANCE

Work is no longer a stage for proving the self.

It becomes a way of participating in the unfolding of reality.

Work becomes:

- focused
- meaningful
- aligned
- steady

The quality of work deepens because the one doing the work is no longer divided.

Work becomes a form of presence.

CREATIVITY AS FLOW OF THE REAL

Creativity becomes fluid when the mind is no longer obstructed by fear or selfconcern.

Creativity is no longer an attempt to express the self.

It is the Real expressing itself through form.

Creativity becomes:

- intuitive

- spacious
- authentic
- unforced

The creative act becomes a revelation, not a performance.

DIFFICULTY WITHOUT SUFFERING

Difficulty remains.

Suffering changes.

Difficulty is part of the unfolding of life.

Suffering is the resistance to that unfolding.

When the Real is the ground:

- difficulty is met directly
- resistance dissolves
- fear softens
- clarity remains

Pain is felt, but it is not amplified by narrative.

Difficulty becomes a teacher, not an enemy.

JOY WITHOUT REASON

Joy emerges as a quiet undercurrent—not tied to events, achievements, or circumstances.

Joy arises from:

- alignment
- presence
- unity
- clarity

This joy is not excitement.

It is depth.

It is the natural fragrance of a life lived from the Real.

LIVING AS TRANSPARENCY

To live from the Real is to live transparently—not hiding, not performing, not defending.

Transparency is:

- honesty without aggression
- openness without vulnerability
- presence without pretense

Transparency is not weakness.
It is strength without armor.

THE REAL AS THE FOUNDATION OF LIFE

Living from the Real means:

- seeing clearly
- acting precisely
- loving deeply
- speaking honestly
- resting fully
- meeting life as it is

Life becomes coherent.
Life becomes intimate.
Life becomes whole.
This is not a spiritual state.
It is the natural state when illusion dissolves.

SUMMARY

- The descent from the summit is the expression of clarity in daily life.
- The old center dissolves; being becomes the axis.
- Action becomes unforced and precise.
- Speech becomes simple and compassionate.
- Relationship becomes presence meeting presence.
- Work becomes participation, not performance.
- Creativity becomes flow, not effort.
- Difficulty remains, but suffering dissolves.
- Joy becomes a quiet undercurrent.
- Living from the Real is living transparently and coherently.

29

THE HUMAN AS VESSEL OF THE REAL

WHEN A PERSON BEGINS to live from the Real, something subtle yet profound unfolds.

Life does not become extraordinary.

Life becomes *true*.

The human being becomes a vessel—not in the sense of being filled with something foreign, but in the sense of becoming transparent to what was always the ground of their existence.

This chapter explores how the Infinite expresses itself through a human life that no longer resists, distorts, or obscures its own depth.

THE HUMAN AS A CLEARING FOR THE INFINITE

A human being is not a container.

A human being is a clearing—an opening through which the Real can appear in form.

When the illusions of separation dissolve, this clearing becomes unobstructed.

The Infinite does not enter the person.

The Infinite expresses itself *through* the person.

The human becomes:

- a space of clarity
- a space of presence
- a space of compassion
- a space of coherence

This is not mystical.

It is natural.

It is what happens when the mind no longer stands in its own way.

THE DISAPPEARANCE OF INNER CONFLICT

Inner conflict is the friction between illusion and reality.

When illusion dissolves, conflict dissolves with it.

The human being becomes internally unified:

- thought aligns with being
- action aligns with clarity
- emotion aligns with truth
- intention aligns with presence

This does not mean perfection.

It means coherence.

The person is no longer divided against themselves.

THE EMERGENCE OF NATURAL AUTHORITY

Authority does not come from power, position, or knowledge.

Authority arises from alignment with the Real.

A person who lives from the Real carries a quiet authority—not over others, but within themselves.

This authority is:

- calm
- grounded
- unforced
- unmistakable

It is the authority of someone who does not speak from ego, but from clarity.

This authority is not claimed.

It is recognized.

THE HUMAN AS A CONDUIT OF COMPASSION

Compassion deepens when the illusion of separation dissolves.

The suffering of others is no longer "their" suffering.

It is the suffering of being itself.

Compassion becomes:

- instinctive
- steady
- courageous
- clear

It is not sentimental.

It is not indulgent.

It is not selfsacrificing.

It is the natural response of the Real recognizing itself in another form.

THE HUMAN AS A MIRROR OF THE REAL

A person who lives from the Real becomes a mirror—not reflecting their own identity, but reflecting the depth of being.

Others feel:

- seen
- understood
- accepted
- unthreatened

Not because the person is special, but because the person is transparent.

THE REAL SHINES THROUGH THEM.

This is why sages, saints, and awakened beings throughout history have had the same effect:

They do not show themselves.
They show the Real.

THE SIMPLICITY OF A LIFE ALIGNED WITH GOD

When God is recognized as the ground of being, life becomes simple—not easy, but simple.

Simplicity means:

- no unnecessary conflict
- no unnecessary striving
- no unnecessary identity
- no unnecessary fear

Life becomes direct.
Life becomes honest.
Life becomes clear.
This simplicity is not minimalism.

It is truthfulness.

THE HUMAN AS PARTICIPANT IN THE REAL

A person who lives from the Real does not withdraw from the world.

They participate in it more fully.

Participation becomes:

- wholehearted
- present
- responsive
- unburdened

The person does not act to protect the self.

They act to express the Real.

This participation is not passive.

It is deeply engaged.

THE END OF PRETENDING

Pretending is the attempt to appear as something other than what one is.

It is the performance of identity.

When the Real becomes the ground, pretending becomes impossible.

The person becomes:

- authentic without effort
- honest without aggression
- open without vulnerability
- present without performance

This is not a moral achievement.

It is the natural state when illusion dissolves.

THE HUMAN AS A LIVING ANSWER

The question "Who is God?" is no longer answered in words.

It is answered in being.

A person who lives from the Real becomes a living answer—not because they explain God, but because they embody the clarity that God is the ground of all things.

Their life becomes:

- a demonstration
- a revelation
- a transparency
- a presence

The Infinite becomes visible in the finite.

THE THRESHOLD BEFORE THE FINAL DESCENT

This chapter marks the deepening of embodiment—the moment where the human being becomes a vessel of the Real, a living expression of God's existence.

The next chapter will explore the final descent:

how a life grounded in the Real moves through the world, through time, through relationships, and through mortality with unshakable clarity.

SUMMARY

- A human being becomes a clearing for the Infinite when illusion dissolves.
- Inner conflict disappears as the self becomes coherent.
- Natural authority arises from alignment with the Real.
- Compassion becomes instinctive and clear.
- The person becomes a mirror of the Real for others.

- Life becomes simple, direct, and truthful.
- Participation in the world becomes wholehearted and unburdened.
- Pretending falls away; authenticity becomes natural.
- The human becomes a living answer to the question of God.
- This chapter prepares for the final descent into the world.

30

THE STRUCTURE OF A LIFE GROUNDED IN THE REAL

WHEN THE REAL IS recognized as the ground of God, the ground of the self, and the ground of reality, the question of human life must be reconsidered.

Not psychologically.

Not morally.

Not spiritually.

Ontologically.

This chapter examines the structural implications of living from the Real—how the recognition of the Infinite reorganizes the architecture of human existence.

It is not a call.

It is a clarification.

THE ONTOLOGICAL SHIFT FROM IDENTITY TO BEING

The first structural change is the relocation of the center of life.

Identity is a construct.
Being is foundational.
Identity depends on:

- memory
- narrative
- comparison
- social reflection
- psychological continuity

Being depends on nothing.
It is the ground from which identity arises.
When the Real becomes clear, the human being no longer lives from identity.
Identity remains functional, but it ceases to be existential.
This shift is not psychological.
It is ontological.

THE RECONFIGURATION OF ACTION

Action changes when its source changes.
When action arises from identity, it is driven by:

- fear
- desire
- selfprotection
- selfenhancement
- social positioning

When action arises from being, it is driven by:

- clarity
- coherence
- appropriateness
- responsiveness
- presence

The structure of action becomes nonreactive.

It becomes aligned with the Real rather than with the egoic narrative.

This does not make action passive.

It makes action precise.

THE TRANSFORMATION OF MOTIVATION

Motivation is the internal architecture of action.

It reveals the axis around which life turns.

When the self is believed to be separate, motivation is compensatory.

It attempts to secure what the self believes it lacks.

When the Real is recognized, motivation becomes expressive.

It expresses what is already whole.

The shift is from:

- acquisition → expression
- defense → participation
- becoming → being

Motivation becomes transparent to the ground of being.

THE CLARIFICATION OF RELATIONSHIP

Relationship is reinterpreted when the illusion of separateness dissolves.

The other is no longer:

- a threat
- a resource
- a mirror
- a competitor
- an extension of the self

The other is recognized as another expression of the same ground.

This recognition does not erase difference.

It contextualizes it.

Relationship becomes the meeting of two expressions of the Real within the field of being.

This is not sentiment.

It is ontology.

THE REORIENTATION OF TIME

Time is experienced differently when the Real becomes the ground.

The psychological structure of time—anticipation, regret, projection—depends on the belief in a separate self moving through a linear sequence.

When the Real is recognized:

- the present becomes primary
- the future becomes open
- the past becomes contextual
- time becomes a dimension of unfolding, not a burden of identity

This does not eliminate planning or memory.

It removes their existential weight.

Time becomes functional, not foundational.

THE DISSOLUTION OF EXISTENTIAL FEAR

Existential fear arises from the belief that the self is separate, fragile, and threatened by nonbeing.

When the Real is recognized as the ground of being:

- death is reinterpreted
- loss is recontextualized

- uncertainty is depersonalized
- vulnerability is reframed

Fear does not disappear as an emotion.
It dissolves as an ontology.
The self is no longer the locus of existence.
Being is.

THE EMERGENCE OF INNER COHERENCE

Inner coherence is the alignment of thought, emotion, and action with the ground of being.

Coherence arises when:

- illusion dissolves
- contradiction resolves
- fragmentation ends
- the self is no longer divided

Coherence is not perfection.
It is unity of orientation.
The human being becomes internally noncontradictory.
This is the structural consequence of clarity.

THE TRANSPARENCY OF THE WORLD

The world becomes transparent to its ground.

Objects remain objects.

Events remain events.

People remain people.

But the world is no longer interpreted as a collection of independent entities.

It is understood as the continuous expression of the Real.

This transparency is not mystical.

It is ontological.

The world is seen in its depth.

THE HUMAN AS EXPRESSION, NOT EXCEPTION

The human being is no longer imagined as an exception within reality.

The human being is recognized as an expression of the same ground that expresses stars, trees, rivers, and galaxies.

This recognition does not diminish humanity.

It situates humanity.

The human becomes:

- finite in form
- infinite in ground
- unique in expression
- unified in essence

This is the structural truth of existence.

THE ARCHITECTURE OF A LIFE GROUNDED IN THE REAL

A life grounded in the Real is characterized by:

- being rather than identity
- clarity rather than belief
- coherence rather than conflict
- presence rather than projection
- expression rather than acquisition
- unity rather than separation
- transparency rather than performance

This is not an ideal.

It is the natural structure of life when illusion dissolves.

THE THRESHOLD BEFORE THE FINAL VISION

This chapter completes the philosophical articulation of embodiment—the structural consequences of recognizing the Real as the ground of existence.

31

THE IMPLICATIONS OF LIVING FROM THE REAL

WHEN THE REAL BECOMES the ground of human life, the implications extend beyond the individual.

They reshape the entire framework through which the human being interprets the world.

This chapter examines these implications in a philosophical manner—not as prescriptions, but as structural consequences of clarity.

The human being does not merely change internally.

The human being's *relation* to everything changes.

THE REINTERPRETATION OF THE WORLD

The world is no longer perceived as a collection of independent objects.

It is understood as a continuous field of being.

This reinterpretation has several implications:

- objects are contextualized within the whole
- events are understood as expressions of underlying processes
- systems are seen as interdependent
- boundaries are recognized as functional, not absolute

The world becomes intelligible not through fragmentation, but through coherence.

This coherence is not imposed by the mind.

It is discovered in the structure of reality itself.

THE REORIENTATION OF KNOWLEDGE

Knowledge shifts from accumulation to understanding.

Accumulation is quantitative.

Understanding is qualitative.

Accumulation seeks more information.

Understanding seeks deeper insight.

When the Real is the ground:

- knowledge becomes relational
- truth becomes contextual
- interpretation becomes transparent
- certainty becomes unnecessary

Knowledge is no longer a possession of the self.

It is a participation in the intelligibility of being.

This reorientation dissolves the anxiety that once accompanied the pursuit of certainty.

THE TRANSFORMATION OF VALUE

Value is no longer derived from scarcity, competition, or social validation.

Value arises from alignment with the Real.

This transforms the structure of value:

- worth is not comparative
- meaning is not constructed
- significance is not assigned
- importance is not negotiated

Value becomes intrinsic to being.
This intrinsic value is not subjective.
It is ontological.

THE CLARIFICATION OF ETHICS

Ethics is no longer grounded in rules, consequences, or cultural norms.

It is grounded in ontology.
Ethical clarity arises when:

- the self is understood as nonseparate
- the other is recognized as expression of the same ground
- action is aligned with coherence
- harm is understood as distortion of being

Ethics becomes the natural consequence of unity.
This does not eliminate moral complexity.
It reframes it.
Ethics becomes a matter of alignment, not obedience.

THE REFRAMING OF SOCIETY

Society is reinterpreted when the illusion of separateness dissolves.

Society is not a collection of individuals.
It is a network of expressions of the Real.
This reframing has structural implications:

- cooperation becomes more natural than competition
- conflict becomes a symptom of misalignment

- institutions become expressions of collective being
- culture becomes a field of shared meaning

Society is no longer understood as a battleground of interests.
It becomes a system of interdependent expressions.
This reframing does not idealize society.
It clarifies its nature.

THE REINTERPRETATION OF SUFFERING

Suffering is no longer interpreted as personal failure or cosmic injustice.

It is understood as the friction between illusion and reality.
This reinterpretation has several implications:

- suffering becomes intelligible
- resistance becomes visible
- healing becomes alignment
- compassion becomes natural

Suffering remains real.
But its meaning changes.
It becomes part of the process through which clarity emerges.

THE RECONTEXTUALIZATION OF DEATH

Death is no longer the negation of being.

It is the transformation of form within the same ground.
This recontextualization dissolves existential anxiety:

- death is not annihilation
- death is not separation
- death is not loss of being

Death becomes a structural feature of finite expression.
This does not trivialize death.

It situates it.

THE HUMAN AS A NODE OF THE REAL

A human being becomes a node—a point of articulation—within the field of being.

This has several implications:

- individuality is preserved as expression
- unity is preserved as ground
- agency is preserved as participation
- responsibility is preserved as coherence

The human is neither isolated nor dissolved.

The human is contextualized.

This contextualization is the philosophical resolution of the tension between individuality and unity.

THE EMERGENCE OF A NEW ORIENTATION

When the Real becomes the ground, a new orientation emerges:

- from separation to participation
- from identity to being
- from accumulation to understanding
- from control to alignment
- from fear to clarity

This orientation is not a choice.

It is the natural consequence of recognition.

32

THE UNITY OF EXISTENCE

When the Real is recognized as the ground of all things, the structure of existence itself becomes intelligible in a new way.

The world is no longer a set of discrete entities.

The self is no longer an isolated subject.

God is no longer a distant hypothesis.

Existence reveals itself as a unified field—differentiated in form, but undivided in essence.

This chapter examines the philosophical implications of this unity.

THE GROUND AS THE SINGLE PRINCIPLE OF REALITY

Every metaphysical system seeks a first principle—a foundation from which all else follows.

In the clarity of the Real, this principle is not conceptual but ontological.

The ground of being is:

- unconditioned
- indivisible
- selfexistent
- foundational

It is not one entity among others.

It is the condition for the possibility of all entities.

This ground is what theology calls God, what philosophy calls Being, and what experience reveals as presence.

The unity of existence begins here.

DIFFERENTIATION WITHOUT DIVISION

Existence displays infinite differentiation—galaxies, organisms, minds, cultures, identities.

But differentiation does not imply division.

Division is a conceptual overlay.

Differentiation is an ontological fact.

The Real expresses itself through:

- multiplicity of forms
- diversity of phenomena
- complexity of systems
- individuality of beings

But the ground remains one.

Unity is not sameness.

Unity is shared origin.

THE STRUCTURE OF MANIFESTATION

Manifestation is the process through which the Real appears as form.

This process is not temporal but structural.

Manifestation involves:

- potential becoming actual
- ground becoming expression
- being becoming appearance
- unity becoming multiplicity

This is not a transformation of the Real.
It is the articulation of the Real.
The Real does not change.
Form changes.
This distinction is essential for understanding the unity of existence.

THE SELF AS A LOCALIZED EXPRESSION OF THE REAL

The human self is a localized point of articulation within the field of being.
It is neither autonomous nor illusory.
It is a finite expression of an infinite ground.
This has several implications:

- consciousness is not produced by the self
- identity is not the essence of the self
- individuality is not separation
- agency is participation, not independence

The self is real as expression, not as foundation.

THE WORLD AS THE FIELD OF EXPRESSION

The world is not external to the self.
It is the broader field in which the self participates.
The world is:

- relational

- interdependent
- dynamic
- coherent

The unity of existence becomes visible when the world is understood as the continuous articulation of the Real.

The world is not a stage.

It is a manifestation.

GOD AS THE DEPTH OF THE REAL

The concept of God becomes clarified when the Real is recognized as the ground of being.

God is not:

- a separate agent
- a cosmic ruler
- an external creator

God is:

- the depth of existence
- the ground of being
- the unity of all things
- the source of manifestation

This is not a reduction of God.

It is the philosophical purification of the concept.

God is the Real understood in its absolute dimension.

THE UNITY OF GOD, SELF, AND WORLD

When the ground is recognized as the single principle of reality, the apparent distinctions between God, self, and world become structural rather than absolute.

- God is the ground.
- The self is a localized expression.
- The world is the field of expression.

These are not three separate domains.
They are three aspects of one reality.
The unity of existence is the recognition that all distinctions are internal to the Real.

THE RESOLUTION OF DUALITIES

Classical metaphysics is structured around dualities:

- subject and object
- mind and world
- sacred and secular
- finite and infinite
- immanent and transcendent

In the clarity of the Real, these dualities are reinterpreted.
They are not contradictions.
They are complementary aspects of a single field.
The Real is both immanent and transcendent.
The self is both finite and grounded in the infinite.
The world is both differentiated and unified.
Dualities dissolve into polarity.
Polarity dissolves into unity.

THE COHERENCE OF EXISTENCE

When unity becomes clear, existence reveals a deep coherence:

- phenomena arise from the same ground
- processes unfold within the same field

- beings participate in the same reality
- meaning emerges from the same source

Coherence is not imposed by the mind.
It is discovered in the structure of being.
This coherence is the philosophical signature of the Real.

33

THE COHERENCE OF GOD, SELF, AND WORLD

When the Real is recognized as the ground of existence, the apparent complexity of reality begins to resolve into a coherent structure.

This coherence is not imposed by thought.

It is discovered in the nature of being itself.

This chapter articulates the philosophical coherence that emerges when God, self, and world are understood as differentiated expressions of a single ontological ground.

THE NECESSITY OF A SINGLE GROUND

A coherent metaphysics requires a single foundational principle.

Multiple independent principles create fragmentation.

A single ground creates unity.

The Real functions as this ground because it is:

- unconditioned
- selfexistent
- indivisible
- ontologically prior

Everything that exists participates in this ground.
Nothing exists independently of it.
This necessity is not dogmatic.
It is structural.

THE THREEFOLD STRUCTURE OF EXPRESSION

Existence expresses itself in three primary modes:

- *the ground (God)*
- *the localized expression (self)*
- *the field of manifestation (world)*

These are not three substances.
They are three aspects of one reality.
This threefold structure is not hierarchical.
It is relational.
Each aspect is intelligible only in relation to the others.

GOD AS THE ONTOLOGICAL DEPTH

God is the name for the Real understood in its absolute dimension.
Not a being, but the ground of being.
Not an agent, but the condition for agency.
Not a cause, but the foundation of causality.
This understanding resolves classical tensions:

- transcendence and immanence
- unity and multiplicity
- eternity and temporality

God is not outside the world.
God is the depth of the world.

THE SELF AS FINITE LOCALIZATION OF THE INFINITE

The self is a finite center of experience within the field of being.
It is not independent of the ground.
It is not reducible to the ground.
It is a localized articulation of the ground.
This resolves the tension between:

- individuality and unity
- agency and dependence
- freedom and determinism

The self is free insofar as it aligns with the Real.
It is constrained insofar as it identifies with illusion.

THE WORLD AS THE FIELD OF MANIFESTATION

The world is the totality of forms arising within the ground.
It is not separate from the ground.
It is the articulation of the ground in multiplicity.
This resolves the tension between:

- appearance and reality
- matter and spirit
- nature and divinity

The world is not a distraction from the Real.
It is the Real in expression.

THE COHERENCE OF THE THREE

The coherence of God, self, and world becomes evident when they are understood as:

- *ground (God)*
- *expression (self)*
- *manifestation (world)*

These are not competing explanations.
They are complementary dimensions of one reality.
The Real is the unity that holds them together.

THE RESOLUTION OF CLASSICAL PHILOSOPHICAL PROBLEMS

When the unity of existence is recognized, several longstanding philosophical problems dissolve:

- *Mind–body problem: mind and body are two modes of the same ground.*
- *Free will vs. determinism: freedom is alignment with being; determinism is misalignment.*
- *Problem of universals: universals are structural features of the ground.*
- *Problem of the one and the many: the many are expressions of the one.*
- *Problem of God's relation to the world: God is the depth of the world, not external to it.*

These problems were generated by the assumption of separateness.
They dissolve when unity becomes the foundation.

THE COHERENCE OF MEANING

Meaning is no longer constructed.

Meaning is discovered.
Meaning arises from:

- participation in the ground
- alignment with being
- recognition of unity
- expression of the Real

Meaning is not subjective or objective.
It is relational.
It emerges from the relation between finite expression and infinite ground.

THE COHERENCE OF ETHICS

Ethics becomes coherent when grounded in ontology.
Ethical clarity arises when:

- the self is understood as nonseparate
- the other is recognized as expression of the same ground
- action is aligned with coherence
- harm is understood as distortion of being

Ethics is not imposed.
It is revealed.
It is the natural consequence of unity.

THE COHERENCE OF EXISTENCE

Existence becomes coherent when:

- God is understood as ground
- the self is understood as expression
- the world is understood as manifestation

This coherence is not conceptual.

It is structural.
It is the architecture of reality itself.

34

THE REAL AS THE FINAL EXPLANATORY PRINCIPLE

When the unity of existence becomes clear, the question that remains is not *what* reality is, but *why* reality is intelligible at all.

This chapter examines the Real as the final explanatory principle—the foundation that makes existence coherent, meaning possible, and understanding attainable.

The Real is not merely the ground of being.

It is the ground of intelligibility.

THE NEED FOR AN EXPLANATORY PRINCIPLE

Every philosophical system requires an ultimate explanatory principle—a point beyond which explanation cannot proceed without circularity or regress.

Such a principle must be:

- selfexistent
- nonderivative

- noncomposite
- ontologically prior
- universally applicable

The Real satisfies these criteria because it is not one entity among others.

It is the condition for the possibility of all entities.

This is not an assumption.

It is a structural necessity.

THE REAL AS THE CONDITION FOR INTELLIGIBILITY

Intelligibility requires coherence.

Coherence requires unity.

Unity requires a single ground.

The Real provides this ground by functioning as:

- the source of being
- the source of order
- the source of relation
- the source of meaning

Without the Real, existence would be a collection of unrelated facts.

With the Real, existence becomes a coherent field.

Intelligibility is not imposed on reality.

It emerges from the structure of the Real.

THE REAL AS THE BASIS OF CAUSALITY

Causality is not merely the succession of events.

It is the expression of underlying continuity.

The Real provides this continuity by:

- grounding the persistence of entities
- enabling the interaction of forms
- sustaining the coherence of processes

Causality is not external to the Real.

It is the articulation of the Real in time.

This resolves the classical tension between determinism and freedom:

determinism describes the structure of manifestation;

freedom describes the alignment of the self with the ground.

THE REAL AS THE BASIS OF MEANING

Meaning is not subjective projection.

Meaning is the recognition of relation within a unified field.

Meaning arises when:

- the self recognizes its participation in the ground
- the world is seen as expression of the ground
- God is understood as the depth of the ground

Meaning is not constructed.

Meaning is discovered.

The Real is the condition for meaning because it is the unity that makes relation possible.

THE REAL AS THE BASIS OF TRUTH

Truth is correspondence between thought and reality.

But correspondence requires a stable ground.

The Real provides this ground by:

- being selfidentical
- being noncontradictory

- being the source of all forms
- being the measure of coherence

Truth is not arbitrary.
Truth is grounded in the structure of being.
The Real is the criterion of truth because it is the foundation of all that exists.

THE REAL AS THE BASIS OF VALUE

Value is not created by preference.
Value emerges from alignment with being.
The Real grounds value by:

- providing intrinsic worth to all expressions
- situating individuality within unity
- revealing harm as distortion of coherence
- revealing goodness as alignment with the ground

Value is not subjective or objective.
It is ontological.
The Real is the source of value because it is the source of existence.

THE REAL AS THE BASIS OF UNITY

Unity is not the elimination of difference.
Unity is the recognition of shared ground.
The Real unifies:

- God as depth
- self as expression
- world as manifestation

These are not separate domains.
They are differentiated aspects of one reality.

Unity is not a metaphysical claim.
It is the structure of existence.

THE REAL AS THE BASIS OF DIVERSITY

Diversity is not a threat to unity.

It is the articulation of unity.

The Real expresses itself through:

- multiplicity of forms
- complexity of systems
- individuality of beings
- variation of phenomena

Diversity is not accidental.
It is essential to manifestation.
Unity is the ground.
Diversity is the expression.

THE REAL AS THE FINAL CONTEXT

Every question—metaphysical, ethical, existential—ultimately resolves into the Real.

The Real is:

- the context of God
- the context of self
- the context of world
- the context of meaning
- the context of truth
- the context of value

The Real is not one part of reality.
It is the context in which reality appears.

35

THE FINAL INTEGRATION

Existence as the Real

THE PHILOSOPHICAL ARCHITECTURE IS now complete.

The distinctions between God, self, and world have been clarified, contextualized, and unified.

The Real has been established as the ground of being, the condition of intelligibility, and the final explanatory principle.

This chapter integrates the entire system into a single, coherent vision of existence.

THE REAL AS THE ABSOLUTE GROUND

The Real is the foundation upon which all metaphysical categories depend.

It is not an entity within reality.

It is the condition for the possibility of reality.

The Real is:

- unconditioned
- selfexistent

- indivisible
- ontologically prior

Everything that exists participates in the Real.
Nothing exists independently of it.
This is the absolute ground of existence.

GOD AS THE DEPTH OF THE REAL

The concept of God becomes intelligible when understood as the depth dimension of the Real.

God is:

- not a being
- not an agent
- not an external creator

God is:

- the depth of being
- the unity of existence
- the source of manifestation
- the ground of intelligibility

God is the Real in its absolute aspect.

This resolves the tension between transcendence and immanence:

God is transcendent as ground, immanent as depth.

THE SELF AS FINITE EXPRESSION OF THE REAL

The self is neither autonomous nor illusory.

It is a finite articulation of the infinite ground.

The self is:

- localized
- embodied
- perspectival
- relational

Its individuality is real as expression, not as foundation.
This resolves the tension between freedom and determinism:
freedom is alignment with the Real;
determinism is the structure of manifestation.
The self is not separate from the Real.
It is a mode of the Real.

THE WORLD AS MANIFESTATION OF THE REAL

The world is not external to the ground.
It is the articulation of the ground in multiplicity.
The world is:

- coherent
- relational
- dynamic
- intelligible

Its diversity is not a challenge to unity.
It is the expression of unity.
This resolves the tension between appearance and reality:
appearance is the Real in form;
reality is the Real in depth.

THE UNITY OF GOD, SELF, AND WORLD

The unity of existence becomes clear when the three primary aspects of reality are understood as differentiated expressions of a single ground:

- *God—the depth of the Real*
- *Self—the localized expression of the Real*
- *World—the field of manifestation of the Real*

These are not separate domains.
They are structural dimensions of one reality.
Unity is not a metaphysical claim.
It is the architecture of being.

THE COHERENCE OF EXISTENCE

Existence becomes coherent when grounded in the Real.

Coherence arises because:

- being is unified
- manifestation is structured
- relation is intrinsic
- intelligibility is grounded
- meaning is relational
- value is ontological

Coherence is not imposed by thought.
It is discovered in the structure of reality.
The Real is the principle of coherence.

THE RESOLUTION OF METAPHYSICAL TENSIONS

The system resolves classical philosophical tensions by situating them within the unity of the Real:

- *One and many—unity as ground, multiplicity as expression*
- *Mind and world—two modes of the same field*
- *Finite and infinite—finite as articulation of the infinite*
- *Immanent and transcendent—two aspects of the Real*

- *Freedom and determinism—freedom as alignment, determinism as structure*
- *Appearance and reality—appearance as manifestation, reality as depth*

These tensions dissolve when the Real becomes the foundation.

THE REAL AS THE FINAL CONTEXT OF UNDERSTANDING

All questions—metaphysical, ethical, existential—ultimately resolve into the Real.

The Real is:

- the context of God
- the context of self
- the context of world
- the context of meaning
- the context of truth
- the context of value
- the context of existence

The Real is not one part of reality.
It is the context in which reality appears.
This is the final integration.

THE COMPLETION OF THE SYSTEM

The metaphysical architecture is now complete:

- The Real is the ground.
- God is the depth.
- The self is the expression.
- The world is the manifestation.

- Unity is the structure.
- Coherence is the signature.
- Meaning is the relation.
- Existence is the articulation of the Real.

Nothing lies outside this framework.
Nothing needs to be added.
Nothing can be removed without collapsing the system.
This is the philosophical completion of the book.

CLOSING REFLECTION

The Real as the Simple Fact of Existence

THE INQUIRY HAS REACHED its limit.

Not because there is nothing more to say, but because further elaboration would no longer deepen understanding.

Every concept has been traced to its ground.

Every distinction has been contextualized.

Every tension has been resolved within the unity of the Real.

What remains is a single, stable recognition:

Existence is grounded in the Real, and nothing stands outside it.

This is not a conclusion.

It is the point at which explanation becomes unnecessary.

THE SIMPLICITY BENEATH THE ARCHITECTURE

The metaphysical structure developed throughout this work is intricate, but the reality it describes is simple.

The Real is:

- the ground of being
- the depth of God
- the essence of the self
- the unity of the world

These are not four truths.
They are four perspectives on one truth.
The complexity lies in the articulation.
The simplicity lies in the fact.

THE REAL AS THE CONSTANT

Throughout every stage of inquiry—conceptual, existential, metaphysical—the Real has remained unchanged.

It is:

- prior to thought
- prior to identity
- prior to world
- prior to God as concept

The Real is the constant that makes all variation possible.
It is the silent background against which all forms arise.

THE TRANSPARENCY OF EXISTENCE

When the Real is recognized, existence becomes transparent to its ground.

Transparency does not eliminate form.
It reveals the depth within form.
The world does not disappear.
It becomes intelligible.
The self does not dissolve.
It becomes contextualized.
God does not retreat.

God becomes clear.
Transparency is the final mode of understanding.

THE END OF METAPHYSICAL URGENCY

The search for ultimate explanation ends not in certainty, but in clarity.

Certainty belongs to belief.
Clarity belongs to being.
Clarity does not resolve every question.
It dissolves the need for resolution.
The urgency that once drove inquiry is replaced by coherence.
The system holds.

THE REAL AS THE QUIET FOUNDATION

The Real does not demand affirmation.

It does not require assent.
It does not depend on recognition.
It is simply the case.

The Real is the quiet foundation beneath all experience—the unnoticed condition that makes noticing possible.

It is the fact that remains when all interpretations fall away.

THE COMPLETION OF THE INQUIRY

The inquiry is complete because its aim has been fulfilled:

- to identify the ground of existence
- to clarify the relation between God, self, and world
- to articulate the unity beneath multiplicity
- to reveal the coherence of being
- to situate human life within this structure

Nothing further is required.

The architecture stands on its own.

THE FINAL THOUGHT

If one were to reduce the entire work to a single philosophical statement, it would be this:

The Real is the ground of all that exists, and everything is an expression of that ground.

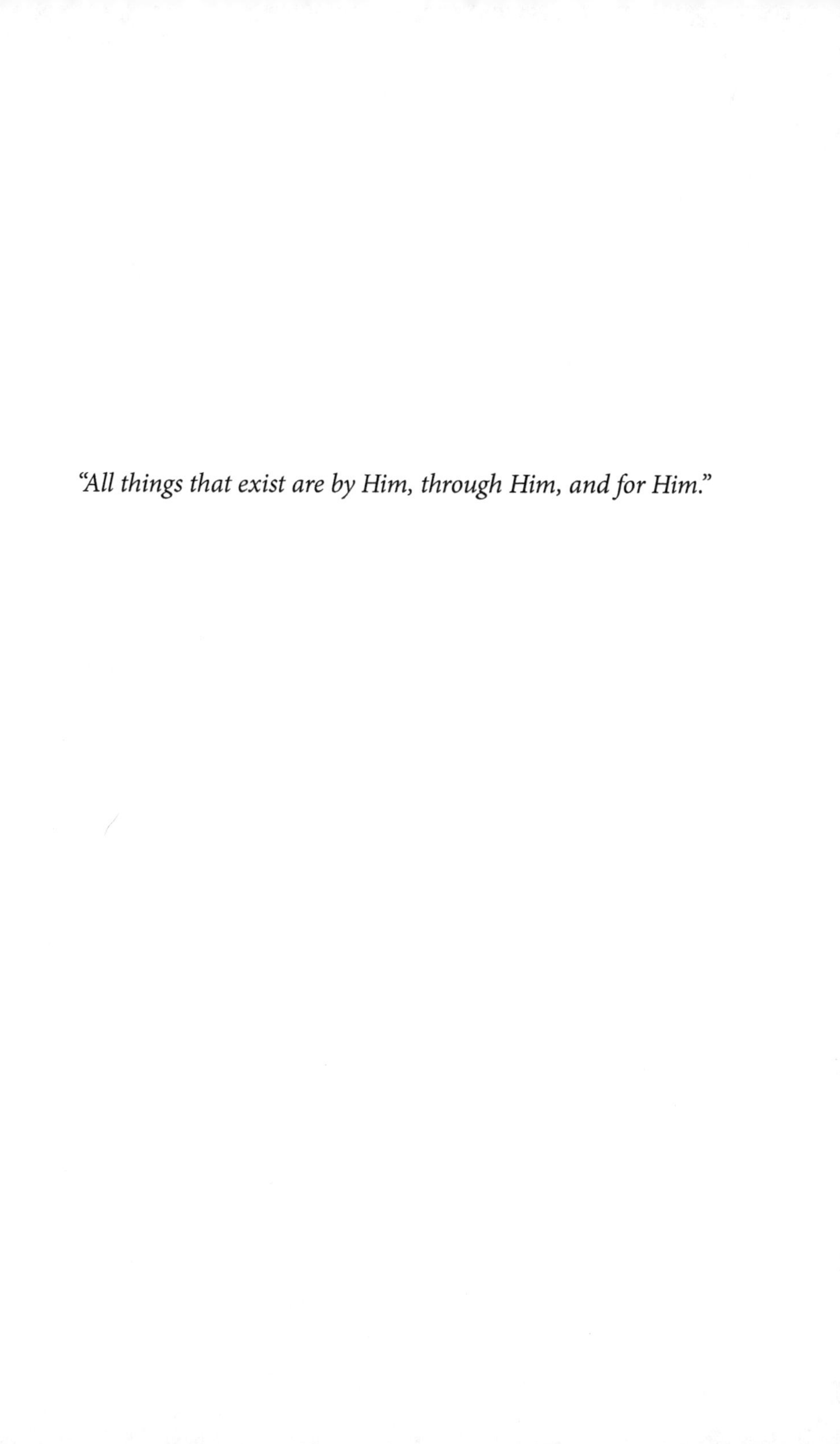

"All things that exist are by Him, through Him, and for Him."

Author Biography

Conde Cagalitan is a philosopher-author whose work explores the structure of existence, the nature of the Real, and the unity of God, self, and world. His writing integrates metaphysics, ontology, and existential analysis into a coherent architectural vision of reality. Working at the intersection of classical theism and contemporary philosophical inquiry, he seeks to clarify the ground of being and the conditions that make meaning, coherence, and intelligibility possible. His canons aim to restore depth, clarity, and responsibility to the language of ultimate reality.

Acknowledgments

THIS WORK WAS SHAPED by many conversations, questions, and moments of clarity shared across years of inquiry. I am grateful to those who engaged the ideas with seriousness, challenged assumptions, and helped refine the structure that eventually became this book. I also acknowledge the scholars, thinkers, and traditions whose insights formed the broader intellectual landscape in which this work stands. Their contributions, whether direct or indirect, remain part of the ongoing pursuit of understanding the ground of existence.

Notes

THIS WORK IS A philosophical exploration grounded in first-principle reasoning rather than textual analysis. No external sources are quoted or cited directly. The ideas developed here draw broadly from the history of metaphysics, classical theism, and nondual philosophical traditions, but the arguments and formulations presented are original to the author.

Further Reading

CLASSICAL METAPHYSICS AND ONTOLOGY

- Aristotle. *Metaphysics.*
- Plotinus. *The Enneads.*
- Thomas Aquinas. *Summa Theologiae.*
- Meister Eckhart. *Selected Writings.*
- Maimonides. *The Guide for the Perplexed.*

PHILOSOPHICAL THEOLOGY AND THE GROUND OF BEING

- Paul Tillich. *Systematic Theology.*
- Karl Rahner. *Foundations of Christian Faith.*
- David Bentley Hart. *The Experience of God: Being, Consciousness, Bliss.*
- John D. Caputo. *The Mystical Element in Heidegger's Thought.*

NONDUAL AND COMPARATIVE METAPHYSICS

- Shankara. *Crest-Jewel of Discrimination.*
- The Upanishads.
- Lao Tzu. *Tao Te Ching.*
- Nagarjuna. *Fundamental Verses of the Middle Way.*

MODERN AND CONTEMPORARY PHILOSOPHY

- Martin Heidegger. *Being and Time.*
- Jean-Luc Marion. *God Without Being.*
- Henri Bergson. *Creative Evolution.*
- Alfred North Whitehead. *Process and Reality.*

PHILOSOPHY OF RELIGION AND ULTIMATE REALITY

- William James. *The Varieties of Religious Experience.*
- Mircea Eliade. *The Sacred and the Profane.*
- Rudolf Otto. *The Idea of the Holy.*

Glossary of Terms

BEING

The condition of existing as a determinate entity within the world. Being is finite, contingent, and dependent on the Real for its intelligibility. It belongs to creatures, not to God, and is always grounded rather than selfexplanatory.

CONSCIOUSNESS

The capacity for awareness, selfreflection, and intelligibility. Consciousness is the point where the world becomes known and where the Real becomes implicitly present within the finite self.

EXISTENCE

The fact of being present within the world of forms. Existence is not ultimate; it is grounded in the Real. To exist is to participate in a deeper ontological foundation that precedes all appearances and makes them possible.

FORM

The structured appearance of a thing within the world. Form is the way the Real becomes visible in finite terms. It expresses the Real under the conditions of existence without exhausting it.

GOD

Not a being among beings, but the ground of all being. God is the Real understood theologically: the One by whom, through whom, and for whom all things exist. God transcends existence while sustaining it.

GROUND

The ontological basis that makes existence possible. The ground is not an object within the world but the condition that underlies all objects, selves, and phenomena. It is the silent foundation of all being.

IDENTITY

The structured sense of self that arises within existence. Identity is contextual, contingent, and shaped by the world of forms. It is the finite expression of a deeper grounding in the Real.

INTELLIGIBILITY

The capacity of reality to be understood. Intelligibility arises because the Real is coherent and unified. The world can be known because it is grounded in a principle that is itself knowable, even if not exhaustively.

MANIFESTATION

The mode by which the Real appears as world, form, and experience. Manifestation is not separate from the Real but its expression in finite structure. The world is the Real in appearance; the Real is the world in depth.

REALITY

The total field of what appears, including both the world of forms and the ground that sustains them. Reality is intelligible because it is unified by the Real and not divided into independent domains.

THE REAL

The ground of all that exists. The Real is not a being, not an object, and not a concept, but the ontological foundation that makes being, world, and God intelligible. Everything exists by the Real, through the Real, and within the Real.

SELF

The finite center of awareness that experiences the world. The self is not autonomous; it is grounded in the Real and participates in its expression. It is both a form within existence and a point of access to the ground beyond existence.

TRANSPARENCY

The condition in which existence reveals its ground. When the world becomes transparent, the Real is recognized as the foundation of all appearance. Transparency does not eliminate form; it reveals the depth within form.

UNITY

The underlying coherence of God, self, and world. Unity is not sameness but the recognition that all distinctions arise within and are sustained by the Real. Unity is the structural truth of reality.

WORLD

The domain of forms, relations, and appearances. The world is not self-grounding; it is the manifestation of the Real in finite structure. It is the field in which beings appear, act, and relate.

Index

INDEX

www.ingramcontent.com/pod-product-compliance
Lightning Source LLC
LaVergne TN
LVHW050624100826
845148LV00011B/1714

* 9 7 9 8 3 8 5 2 7 9 8 2 1 *